bestfootforward

by Students of

Gainesville Middle School

Edited by

Libby Bicknell

Richard Stafford

S & F Communications of Georgia
P.O. Box 8
Demorest, Georgia 30535

Copyright © 2004 by Libby Bicknell and Richard Stafford

ISBN 0-9650478-7-3 Quality Paperback
Cover Design by Don Bagwell (Concept by Daniel Wellborn)
Technical Assistance by Digital Impact Design, Inc.
Cover Photography by Dick Stafford
First Printing, May 2004
1 2 3 4 5 6 7 8 9 10
PRINTED AND MANUFACTURED IN THE UNITED STATES
by Lightning Source, Inc., a division of Ingram Book Company

U.S.A. $10.00
CAN $13.00

Special thanks to Dr. Sandy Addis of Pioneer RESA; Arts Partner Coordinator, Dr. Kathleen Thompson; Teacher and author, Dr. Gordon Vessells; City of Gainesville Superintendent of Schools, Dr. Steven Ballowe; Grant Coordinator, Christine Brosky; Principal Robert Thorpe; Reading Specialist, Dr. Therese Stewart; and the following teachers who inspired our students to write these narratives: Ms. Bowen, Ms. Filden, Ms. Jackson, Ms. Mady, Ms. Pitre, Ms. Sams, Ms. Unnold, and Ms. Whittemore. Also, thank you to the students who helped type and transfer all the handwritten narratives to book format. But perhaps most importantly, a special thank you to the students of Gainesville Middle School who took on the challenge of interviewing parents, grandparents and neighbors and transforming those interviews into the creative literary works contained within this book. Please note that in most cases the choice of words, the spelling of words and punctuation has been left as written by each student by the editors.

OUR CHARACTER TRAITS

Responsibility	Courage
Respect	Patience
Kindness	Diversity
Integrity	Perseverance
Cooperation	Loyalty

-- The Editors
Ms. Libby Bicknell
Dr. Richard Stafford

Table of Contents of
Our Student Writers

Aryian Gwin	86
Jasper Hale*	48
Sha Harper	39
Kendrick Harris	195
Luke Hickman*	121
Araceli Hidalgo	101
Angie Highsmith	189
Breshana Hill	41
Javon Hill	184
Tanisha Hill	161
Ed Hollis IV	120
Maddie Hollister*	166
Robert Hughes	119
Caoline Jackson*	15
Jonas Jenkins*	71
Niujing Jiang	51
Nicholas Johnson	91
Rayanna Jones	192
Evan King	129
Ashley Kitchel	141
Kunal Lahiry*	186
Rebecca Lawrence*	103
Scott LeFevre	127
Liduvina Leon	57
Renise Lewis	45
Lewis Link	170
Kelsey Maine	55
Edgar Malagon	108
Brandon Mangum	108

Blaine Martin	98
Kelly Mattick*	80
Kiara May*	178
Jasmine Mays	197
Douglas McDuff*	100
D.J. McDuffie	56
Karen Medina	194
Lyndsay Mercer	49
Alexa Miller*	152
Johanna Miller	19
Johnny Millsap	78
Gricelda Miranda	49
Perla Mojica	112
Acencion Molina	73
Elizabeth M. Moore*	126
Elizabeth P. Moore	77
Abby Musselwhite	109
Charlie Newman*	115
Hai Nguyen*	42
Jimmy Nguyen	147
Shari Nguyen	45
Brittany Norman	179
Nayeli Nunez	78
Leslie Odister	31
Norma Olguin*	106
Carla Olivas	177
Stephani Olson	124
Selvi Ortiz	59
Jameisha Osborn*	23

Jack Seals	151
Bianca Serna	83
Jasmine Shealy	21
Angel Shields	61
Sha Shields	110
Matthew Shipman	185
Allison Shuler	158
Lindsey Simpkins	90
Cher Smith*	34
Jaleesa Smith	80
Sequoria Smith	17
Randy Soloman	128
Jordan Stanley	57
Gregory Stenzel	79
Lauren Stewart	175
Patrick Stokey	123
Taylus Storey	41
Kaniesha Stovall	95
Latifah Strickland	52
Demesha Stringer	199
Shamond Stringer*	90
Shi Studivant	186
Christian Summerour	60
Allison Tate	96
Kirston Taylor*	181
Alejandra Tinoco	19
Randy Tran	51
Adam Trotter	24
Charleston Troutman*	110

•*Writers whose stories were selected for inclusion in the musical version of* Best Foot Forward.

CAROLINE JACKSON

The Voice of Big Red
The words kindess, cooperation, and loyalty
Suit my Papa to a "T"

Born during the Great Depression almost 70 years ago
Times were hard, they were poor, but it didn't bring him woe.

Then war was declared when he was just a lad.
Off to Germany to fight Nazis went his dad.

My Papa was excited when the war came to an end
But to the V.A. Hospital went his dad, his friend.

Papa was the man of the house though he didn't want to be
He had to help his mom and show responsibility.

When his dad came home he was different, so angry and sad
Papa had to face the fact that he wasn't the same old dad.

Made fun of, even shot at, my Papa still stood tall.
Then he discovered the a love of his life- the game of football.

He walked across town to watch the games at City Park.
Watching his heroes on the field really lit a spark.

He was inspired by coaches, players, and the roar of the
    crowd.

Soon it was his turn to wear the red jersey and make his
   parents proud.

Coach Deavers taught loyalty and teamwork; Coach Gruhn
   taught him to be strong.
He learned and carried these lessons with him his whole life
   long.

Papa married Memaw in the month of May.
His gridiron lessons followed him as life came play-by-play.

Then it was Papa's turn to be a dad with three elephants in a
   row.
It was time to teach the lessons his coaches did bestow.

He taught them to always do their best and work as a team.
"Keep your feet firmly on the ground but don't forget to
   dream."

No matter what life throws at him, he's an elephant deep
   down inside.
He loves the students and the fans following them far and
   wide.

"Children are our future" so he says and he is there to lend a
   hand.
He believes every elephant can go on to something grand.

He has gotten older now and there's no hair upon his head.

To me, he's just my Papa. To you, he's the Voice of Big Red.

SEQUORIA SMITH

Responsibility

My grandfather grew up in Banks County. He learned responsibility because he had to work at age fifteen. His family was broke in the 1940's, and he quit school and went to work. School was most important so he finished high school when he was grown. When he did go to school, it was a one-room schoolhouse. His first job was at a sawmill, making fifteen dollars a week. He also had a younger brother who worked too, cutting grass. Then he went to the army and after he got out, he moved to Gainesville in 1955. His mother was still in Banks County until 1960 or 1961. That was when his third daughter (my mom) was born.

JUSTIN FORDHAM

Reaping the benefits of living a good life. I, Justin Fordham, spent part of Sunday afternoon talking with my mom about her life growing up. I already knew a lot about it, but today, I asked if she could pinpoint just one person that has impacted her life the most. I had a good idea of who it would be, and I was right. It was my Grandma Ruby.

Let's start by filling in a few blanks. My mom grew up in a small rural community in South Georgia. Even though her parents were not farmers, her grandparents were, and she spent a lot of time with them on their farm. Of course, she had chores at her own home to do, but she also worked a lot with her Papa and Grandma Ruby. My mom might be out helping her papa feeding cows or selling tobacco or she could have been helping Grandma Ruby fix lunch or put up vegetables or jellies.

Grandma Ruby was always patient with my mom or anyone. She always put everyone's needs and concerns before her own. Her life was never too busy to help a friend even if it was just sitting listening or giving asked-for advice. That was just her way and still is.

And then the first year my mom was in college, she got a phone call that her grandparents' house had burned. By the time my mom got there hours later, there were dozens of people who were sorting through what was salvageable from their home. It struck my mom then that all the years of her grandma's love and caring for others was being returned to her in her time of need.

Over the next two days, the house that they had lived in for fifty plus years was completely gone and a foundation for their new home was already started. This only happened because of all the people who were volunteering their time. The people there included anyone from the owner of the tractor company to the president of the bank, to the farm hands that had always worked their farm. My mom could not have imagined this happening had it not been for the love and kindness her grandma Ruby had always shown everyone.

The assortment of people at Grandma Ruby's burned house those two to three days were there because she had always shown each and everyone of them the same love, kindness, and respect. She truly lived, and still lives, the life she tried to teach us. And because of that, at a time in her life when she needed help from others, it was there- she reaped the benefits of her good life.

ALEJANDRA TINOCO

When my father was young, he lived on a farm.
He always fed the animals and did them no harm.
His family also grew food
And his father always told him that his work was very good.
Now my father describes himself
As a responsible self.
My father says he has learned a lot from his young life.
And now he can take care of his job, children, and his wife

JOHANNA MILLER

Thelma Hunter

I wanted to do my project on someone I knew well but not related to me. Mrs. Thelma Hunter is one of Jehovah's Witnesses like me. Mrs. Hunter grew up in Gainesville, GA. She learned many valuable lessons here in Gainesville, GA. She is in her late sixties.

Her mother always taught her to support her family. Her family is very close. This taught her about loyalty. She remembers how her teacher always told her, "to yourself, be true". Mrs.

Hunter explains she could never forget such a strong role model.

When Mrs. Hunter was only twelve, she learned a lot about responsibility. She got a job babysitting one young child. At home, her mother taught her how to clean. She learned to thoroughly do a job so you do not have to go back and redo it. She remembered how everyone in her household had a responsibility.

Mrs. Hunter's grandfather was blind. Before she was one of Jehovah's Witnesses, she attended church. When they went to church one Sunday, he was asked to pray. Mrs. Hunter's friends though it was funny for a blind man to pray. Mrs. Hunter did not think it was funny. She learned to respect all.

In her neighborhood, there was a poor family. Her mother always took old clothes and other needed items to the family. The family consisted of nine children. Now Mrs. Hunter always tries not to be selfish. She learned a good lesson on kindness.

When Mrs. Hunter was little, segregation was still in effect. When the circus came to town, she went with friends. They went to the booth to get hotdogs to snack on. African-Americans were required to leave the area to eat. When they sat down to eat, some lady was loudly saying they should not leave. One woman who overheard the ladies talking said it was okay for them to stay. Mrs. Hunter learned about diversity and the courage to be different.

Mrs. Hunter is very special. She has learned a lot about character. Now, she is a good role model to all younger ones. I learned a lot about her from doing this report, and I hope to learn more in the future.

JASMINE SHEALY

An interview on Caite Beaulieu. This interview is about respect, responsibility, and courage. The first lesson is about respect. The second lesson is about responsibility. Then, it's about courage. Then it's about refreshing your mind.

How did Caite learn about respect? Once, when she was at school, she talked back to her teacher. For her punishment, she had to go to ISS. In ISS, she had to write a page on respect. The page had to be on front and on back. From that day on, she remembered the word respect.

Caite learned the meaning of responsibility on her first job. Her first job was telemarketing. On this job, she had to raise money for politicians. She also had to take calls. Once she didn't take a call, and she got in big trouble. That's how she learned the meaning of responsibility.

How Caite learned the true meaning of courage? She learned the true meaning of courage by her mother. Caite's mother taught her the meaning of courage when she had cancer. While she had cancer, she didn't show fear. That's what really showed the true meaning of courage. Ever since then, she didn't show fear either.

Now it's time for me to refresh your mind. This interview was about how Caite learned the meanings of respect, responsibility, and courage. Caite learned the meaning of respect when she had to write a page on respect. She learned the meaning of responsibility on her first job when she got in trouble for not answering the phone. She learned the meaning of courage when her mother had cancer. That's how she learned the true meanings of respect, responsibility, and courage.

Part 2:

Another interview on Caite Beaulieu. This interview is about the meanings of loyalty, cooperation, patience, and kindness. First lesson is loyalty. The second lesson is cooperation. Next, is patience and kindness. Finally, I will refresh your mind.

Caite gave loyalty when her brother's car broke down. Loyalty in the statement above means how to treat your family. When Caite's brother's car broke down, he called his mother and father for help. Their parents gathered the family together to pitch in and help pay for the car. They had to gather up $1,000. That's how she learned the meaning of loyalty.

Caite's school cooperated when one of the students got cancer. The student was one of Caite's best friends. When the school cooperated when they got the calls. The students, teachers, and parents pitched in and tried to pay it off. The bills added up to be $5,000, but they only raised $3,000. Even though they didn't raise enough money for the bill, the bill got caught up. I guess everything works out for the best. In this paragraph, cooperation means to work together.

Caite learned the meanings of patience and kindness one day by one person. When Caite learned those words was one day after school. This is the whole story of how she learned those two words. Once Caite's teacher stayed after school to help Caite pass a test she was having the next day. Caite thought that her teacher had patience. To Caite, patience means to be slow to anger and understanding other people's problems. Caite's teacher could have gone home and let Caite fail the test. Also, when you give patience, you give kindness. That's how she learned those two words.

This interview was about how Caite learned the meanings of loyalty when her brother's car broke down. She learned the meaning of cooperation when one of her friends got cancer. When she learned the meanings of patience and kindness was when she needed help with the test she was taking the next day. That's how she learned the meanings of loyalty, cooperation, patience, and kindness.

JAMEISHA AND TYSON OSBORN

When I was 8 or 9 years old, I was going to Fair Street, my parents came and got me from school. I knew something was wrong. I kept asking my parents, and they would not say anything. Finally, we got to my great grandmother's house and we called her Moma Bill. Moma Bill was tall, thin, sweet lady, with long beautiful blue-black hair. Moma Bill was Cherokee Indian. I loved going to spend time with my great grandmother, because she always cooked big meals. She also told very funny stories. When I got to the house, I saw all the people there. I saw my grandmother, and she looked upset and was crying. I ran to her and hugged my granny's neck and cried. I was also mad because she left me. A couple of days later, we had the funeral, and I was still mad. I went to bed crying. In my room, I had a chair, and I heard a noise that woke me up. I turned around and looked. There was Moma Bill, sitting in a chair, looking at me and smiling. She told me that it was okay and that she would always be with me, and not to be mad or angry, but to be forgiven and to have patience with those you love and take care of them. Now, to this day, I try to have patience for everyone that comes into my life and try to have good times. But if they do something to hurt me, I always forgive them and tell them I forgive them.

ADAM TROTTER

My mother has done some courageous things. She has turned down smoking, repelled, and helped keep someone from hurting themselves. Courage is an important word. It means even though you were scared, you did something or did not panic. Another word for courage is bravery. Everyone has to have courage in one part of their life.

The first courageous thing my mom has done is turned down smoking. Her family went to visit her grandparents in Alabama. Her cousin lived right down the street from her grandparents. So my mom went over to her cousin's house to play, and her cousin wanted her to smoke. Her cousin said she wished she could stop and that my mom was perfect. My mom said no, and she did not smoke. I think that it was very courageous for her not to smoke with her cousin.

The next courageous thing my mom did was repel down a large rock. She went on a trip called Senior Challenge in high school. She had to do lots of stuff there. She went on a long hike, camped out, and repelled. She said that she was really nervous about the repelling. She said it took about five minutes to finally get the courage to go. When she finally did go, she had a fun time. I would have been pretty nervous about going.

The final courageous thing she did was helped her roommate from hurting herself. Her roommate was threatening to kill herself and hurt herself. My mom tried to calm her down. She got her roommate to stop saying that she was going to kill herself. My mom might have saved her life. That was very courageous.

As you can see, my mom has done some courageous things. There are many other courageous things you can do. Everybody needs courage. If nobody had it, the world would not be as good. I believe that courage is needed throughout the world. Courage is a very powerful emotion.

WRITTEN BY MRS. DAY FOR ALEX GRIER

Perseverence

After taking French classes in high school, I was determined to go to Paris. However, my family did not have enough money to send me. I decided to save my money, so I could send myself

Now a normal person would have gotten a job, but of course, that was too logical for me. I had the bright idea to grow pumpkins from seeds leftover from Halloween. I would grow these pumpkins and sell them on the side of the road. I even envisioned a huge sign that said, "Shelby's Paris Pumpkins".

I remember planting the seeds and waiting patiently for the plants to grow. When the first orange pumpkin appeared, I was so excited. However, my excitement was short-lived. It seems that deer were also excited about my pumpkins. While I was sleeping away in my bed at night, these deer came out and kicked my precious little pumpkins open and ate the insides out! You can imagine my dismay! My dreams of going to Paris were squashed just like my pitiful pumpkins.

After such a traumatic event, I did not give up on my dreams. After getting a job and working my way through college (where I took more French classes), I was finally able to go.

I had gotten a good job after graduating from college and also had a credit card. With these tools on my side, I was on my way! I will never forget my first few steps into that great city. The voices, the people, the scenery- everything was amazing! It was all well worth the wait. My perseverance had finally paid off.

MORGAN BELL

Interviewing my mom

My mom was born July 15, 1963. She was born in Nurnberg, Germany, for 2 years. Then she moved back in 1974. She lived there until 1979. Then in 1983, she moved back until 1986. She went to 3 different high schools. First, she went to Stuttgart American High. Then she went to AFCENT International School. This school has all grades. The last high school she went to was Denbigh High. After school, she had a few responsibilities and they were homework, athletics, and chores. Some chores are cooking dinner, cleaning, laundry, ironing, and babysitting. She also had to work in the yard. There are a few facts about my mom's life.

SHELIZA AGUILERA

When my sister was younger, she had to go to my cousin's house. She would have the patience to be able to play with her Nintendo. I think her job is the best job in the world. Her job is to take care of me. She has the responsibility to make sure I am fine and that nothing will hurt me. My grandmother taught her that you should respect your elders. Give them the respect that you want back in return. She had the courage to tell her dad good-bye when he went off to the war. My sister's best friends, Rachel and Vanessa had the kindness to go to the Humane Society, to go take food for the animals. They take the animals for a walk and give them a bath.

EYLEEN BONILLA

My Mom

My interview with my mom was how to be responsible, kind, cooperative, and respectful to others. My interview focused on how to be respectful to others and have responsibility with people. This is what she told me:

My mom said that she is kind because her parents taught her that way. Being kind has taught her a lot of things. That means that she does not care about people's color, religion, or race. I am kind with whatever person who needs me. That is the way I show kindness.

About responsibility, she said that she likes to be respon-sible on her job, home, and with her only daughter. To be responsible, for example, in her job, she has to be at work each day. At home, I have different responsibilities, like keeping my house clean, cooking dinner, and taking care of my husband and my daughter.

She told me about respect. She said that she respects others. She is respectful, because she does care about what others think about her. She respects people because she wants respect back. She is respectful with whatever person she talks to.

This happened in Honduras about 5 years ago. Hurricane Mitch passed through Honduras. This hurricane did make a disaster of a lot of people's houses.

JENNIFER FULLER

Laura Mae Fuller's Tornado Story

April 6th, 1936, was when I experienced my first tornado. That morning, I went to school especially early. At that time, I had no idea what was happening, I did not even know what a tornado was. That afternoon, when I was picked up from school, the cooperation started.

My neighbors and I had always been close, but in the next week, we became one big family. My family had the only wood burning stove and ice box in the whole neighborhood. The power was out so the expensive electric kitchen items were of no use.

Every evening, our neighbors would come to our house baring different foods for our meals. My mother, being the owner of the wood stove, would prepare supper for all of our family and neighbors. We would sit around the dinner table discussing the issues of sadness and hurt caused by the tornado.

I remember those gloomy days, sad and depressing. I am thankful that we had such good cooperation between friends and family. The memory of the tornado will live inside of me for all times, but since then I have gained internal respect for life and all the things in it. I will always have that.

NIKKI FORTSON

Hard Life

For this paper, I chose to interview my grandpa. He was born in 1947. The first time he learned about responsibility was when he was fifteen years old. His mother had given him the money to give to the rent man when he came by, but instead of giving the rent man the money, he went to the poolroom. Two old men had hustled him for the money, and when he got home, he got three whoopings.

There is one specific chore he has to do in the winter. He has to wake up every morning at five o'clock to make a fire in a potbelly heater. He would have to go get wood and old newspaper in the cold. When it was real cold, you could see the wind coming through the cracks of the door. Through this chore, he learned about responsibility and patience.

I think it was funny when he learned about respect. It was him and four of his friends. They were on the lake, snooping around on other people's property. They had went on this old man's property and ate his peaches, so the police came and got them. He said the peaches were good and cold.

He also learned responsibility when the landlord evicted them from their house. They didn't have any money, so he went to work to help out his family, and he has been working ever since then. He learned about loyalty, too.

He had a lot of courage when the ice storm came. It froze up everything in town. My grandpa had to go out it the cold and chop up some wood. He got frostbite on his toes. That took a lot of courage.

ANTHONY EVANS

Respect
I have respect for you and me,
It can be easy, you will see.
Have respect for the things you see,
Others, self, and property.

I have respect for you and me.
I show others the best in me.
I respect my friends and teachers, too.
It is the proper thing to do.

I have respect for you and me.
I take care of others' property.
I respect the Earth and animals, too,
Respect in everything I do.

I have respect for you and me.
It can be easy, you will see.
Have respect for the things you see,
Others, self, and property.

LESLIE ODISTER

1. When I was eight years old, my dad died. He had been in the hospital for surgery and was getting ready to be released the next day. I was walking with him in the hallway, and he just collapsed. I didn't know what was going on. They wouldn't let me back in his room after that. He died from a blood clot in his lungs. My mom came back with my sister, and I had to be strong for her after that. This taught me courage. My sister and I had to help with the household chores and take on more responsibility. My grandmother showed more courage than any other person I know. I knew that I had to follow in her footsteps if I wanted to help my family.

2. I had my first job when I was twelve years old. I worked in a pizza place on the corner of our street. The money I earned went to buy clothes and help my mom with paying her bills. I'm sure what I gave her didn't put a dent in the bills, but just the knowledge that I helped in some small way gave me a great feeling. This taught me a lot of responsibility.

3. When I moved to Georgia, I was fourteen years old and six months pregnant. We moved here from Los Angeles,

California. This state was like a whole other world. Everything I saw and smelled were different. There wasn't the foggy haze everyday. When I went outside, it didn't smell like exhaust fumes. The people were very friendly, and I didn't have to watch over my back to go for a walk in the neighborhood. The prices of things were so much cheaper, too. I learned a lot about diversity during my first few months here. Everyone may talk different, but they are friendly, too.

4. After my son was born, I decided to move out at the age of fifteen to take care of him and support him on my own. This was not an easy decision. I still had to attend school and send my son to daycare everyday. I was in the 10th grade. Most of my friends had no idea what I had to go through every day. They thought it was cool for me to be living on my own. However, in reality, it was one of the toughest things I have ever done. This was how I learned to persevere.

5. When I was thirteen years old, my cousin and I were eating at McDonald's, close by our house. All of a sudden, people started shooting inside the restaurant. My cousin and I climbed under our table and held hands with our heads down. I thought we were going to die. At the table close by us, we saw someone lying there bleeding, asking fro help. I just closed my eyes. I didn't know what to do. The police came and shot both of the men that were killing people. When my cousin and I got up, there were a lot of people dead. Everyone was crying and screaming. Neither one of us was hurt, but we were both shaken up. I learned that life could end at any moment. Between the death of

my father, and the shooting at McDonald's, I know that I should always live my life to the fullest, and I should never do anything that I might feel guilty about later. You never know when that person may be taken.

LAUREN DALTON

Grandma Dalton on the 1936 Gainesville Tornado

1. Can you think of a story or situation from your youth, in Gainesville, or in your childhood community, which taught you the importance of the words listed above?

THE 1936 Gainesville tornado.

2. Did you have a job or chore or responsibility that helped you understand the word that you picked?

During that time, I was attending Main Street School.

3. Can you remember an incident where another person said or did something that helped you understand one of the words?

There was so much going on and they didn't know which ones were dead and which ones were not, and her mother helped explain everything.

4. Can you think of a family situation or difficulty that taught you the importance of the words listed?

Her teacher was killed during this time, and during this time, it made her very respectful of the weather. It taught her to respect people and help people and so when things happen you can't help it.

CHER SMITH

The Story of Integrity

Charles Reese, a preacher from Atlanta, Georgia, is driving a bus of kids on a mission trip to Columbus, Ohio. The group went to the "projects" there and picked up trash. They also went to parks and planted flowers. Again the next day, they picked up trash. Pastor Reese began to wonder if their work was helping the community. When leaving, the pastor saw a book lying in the middle of the road. As he got closer, he noticed that it was a roll of money. Mr. Reese picked up the money and counted it. There were five-hundred seventy-five dollars; there was four hundred in credit card receipts. The money was from a Chinese restaurant. The pastor asked the group whether he should keep it or not, and many hands were raised. Although, everyone thought that he should share it with the group. Only two kids thought it should be returned. Mr. Reese went to the restaurant and asked for the manager. The manager told him that he had lost the nine hundred seventy five dollars. Charles returned the money to the manager of the restaurant.

That week, the students learned more from the pastor's honesty and integrity than from the mission trip.

JOSIAH BOWERS

Honesty
Interview with Bess Walmsley
Q. What is your definition of honesty?

A. The ability to do the right thing

Q. Tell me how you could show it.
A. The easiest is when someone gives you the wrong change or a lost purse

Q. How do you become honest?
A. It is something taught when you are young, mostly before you mature

Q. Would honesty need for you to capture goals?
A. Your friends found cheating on tests on the internet and you don't participate with them

Q. Could you remember a time you showed honesty?
A. I have found a lost purse and turned it back to the owner.

ANSLEY ADDLESBURGER

Once, when my Aunt Amy was in high school, they had a guest speaker. He had told the students a story about driving when he was drunk.

The guest speaker said that when he was younger, he had gone to a party. There was alcohol being served at the party. He and his friends drank. When he was leaving, he and some of his friends got in his car. He drove the car.

He was driving down the road and didn't stop at the stoplight. A large truck struck the side of the car propelling the vehicle into ongoing traffic where the car was struck again.

As he was talking to the students, they could see that he was in a wheelchair. He told them that he had lost both of his legs in the accident. Along with both his legs being disabled, that night, two of his passengers had been killed. This happened because of his lack of responsibility.

The guest speaker that was at my aunt's high school now travels around the country, telling his story. He is trying to help others try to understand the consequences of his actions. Also, to help them understand that if they make the same mistake, what their own consequences could be.

KEISHA WILMONT

I was raised on a farm in South Georgia. From the time I can remember, I always went to church on Sunday. When I started school, I had to walk a mile to get there. The school was always cold in the winter because we had to wait for the teacher to make a fire in the heater. There were times when we had to keep on our coats, hats, and gloves almost all day long. Sometimes, we didn't have gloves, and our fingers would get so cold, you could hardly stand to touch anything. We'd blow our warm breath on them. My parents moved to another community when I was still in the first year of school, and we didn't have to walk as far to school then, but the school was actually the church and on days when they had a funeral, we had to sit in the back of the church. When we entered in the morning for school, we'd know right away there were going to be a funeral, because they would always put a large black bow on the pew where the person being funeralized used to sit. I would cry all day because it would sadden me to know what someone would be buried that day. I went from 1st grade to 3rd grade. They'd built a new school with all grades under the same roof. The grades were from 1st grade through 12th grade. We also got school buses and we always had to stand up on the bus. Every morning, she would have over 40 people on the bus because she only wanted to make one trip. After school, we had to come and change our clothes and go to the cotton field and pick cotton until almost dark. When we got home from the field, we had to feed the hogs. Then we had to cut wood for the fire and pump the water to take a bath and for the house. And then we had to do our homework, eat, then go to bed. If by chance, we didn't have work, we had to read a book. We couldn't say, "I don't have any homework." By the time I was 12 years old, I was cooking. As a matter of fact, I had a sister one year older and we took turns cooking every morning. If we had a problem in school, the teacher would always send a note by the other one. If the other one didn't sent it, they would get a woopen with the ruler.

NANCY VAZQUEZ

Once there was a girl named Angelica. She went to school walking every day. It was not a long way though. One day Angelica's mom sent her to the store, and she said, "Why can't you send any of my brothers or sisters. Why always me?" And she slammed the door. When she was passing by her uncle's house, she saw somebody standing there looking at her. It was a little boy. She called him a bunch of times, but he didn't answer. He didn't move, walk, laugh, or talk. He looked at my mom. She ran as fast as she could to the store and came home. She told her mom about what had happened, and she said she will never argue with her mom about going to the store ever again.

LEY PUCKETT

Responsibility

One evening, one of my mom's friends and my mom were in the neighbor's yard across the street, playing with sparklers. They would drop the sparklers on the grass and let it catch on fire, then stump the fire out. Then one time, they decided to let the fire get bigger. It got bigger and bigger. They could not put the fire out. My mom ran into her house to find something to put water in to help the situation. The only thing she could find in a hurry was a cereal bowl. My grandmother caught her trying to sneak it out of the house. She asked what my mom was doing with the bowl, and all she could say was "FIRE". She ran and got my grandfather. He came outside, hooked the hose to the outside spigot and put the fire out. By then, my mom's friend had run home, and my mom was left to face the music by herself. Her dad made her knock on the neighbor's door and tell him what she had done. She said it was very embarrassing. She apologized to her neighbor and never played with fire again.

DREW DETTMAN

My mom's responsibilities were very hard but fun, she said. When she didn't do her responsibilities around the farm, she couldn't show her horse. Some of her responsibilities were checking the fences, cleaning stalls, and feeding the animals. My mom said her worst and hardest responsibilities were given to her by both of her parents equally. She said it was fun with some of her responsibilities. Her mom had the most responsibilities. She told me that having her responsibilities made her a better adult. Sometimes, she had to do her brother and sister's chores for them because they were sick. Her weirdest responsibility was hand-raising baby animals of all sorts. For fun, they would ride horses and play tag on horses.

SHA HARPER

On Monique Pierce:

1. When I was young, one of my main situations was watching my younger brothers and sister. While I was doing that, it helped me understand responsibility.

2. My responsibility was taking care of my brother and sisters, since I was the oldest. Taking care of them helped me become responsible. Making sure that they eat, get their homework done, and do other things that they were suppose to do.

3. When my grandmamma use to tell me that taking care of my brothers and sister would help me on down in life. She always use to say things that you do now might help you in life.

4. My family situation was when my mother leave, who will watch the ones that cannot watch themselves? When she left, it was my responsibility to finish what she did not.

5. In my community, cooperation came along when everyone had to work together, to solve an issue. Like when the community were beginning to look like a dumpster. After we work together, and cooperate with each other, everything was alright. It did not affect the community. It help us become stronger.

Life Taught Ahead of Time
Life is always
Going to be here
Whether you need
The right or wrong
Path. Life is
Something that will
Last for a lifetime.
Life is like a roller
Coaster that has
Ups, and downs.
Life is something
That will lead to
Your dreams. Even though
You may not take the
Responsibility in life
For real. No matter
What happens, responsibility,
Cooperation, kindness, respect
And patience is a part of your life.

BRESHANA HILL

Have you ever wondered what the word loyalty means? I know you're probably saying to yourself, all I have to do is look it up in the dictionary, then I will know. No, I'm talking about really understanding what the word means. Well, I didn't until I sat down with my mother, Shannon Hill and listened to her story.

One night, my best friend Tiffany was hanging out with some of her other friends. And they all decided to drink alcoholic beverages. Tiffany took in more than she could handle. The girls thought it was funny, so they left her stranded without a way home. She felt alone and scared. So she called me. I got up and went to go get her.

I explained to her that she had made a very bad decision that night. Tiffany was so thankful that I came and got her when she was in need of my help. And she said that I was a true friend. Until this day, Tiffany and I are still best friends. And I know that if it was me, she would do the same thing.

Now do you understand the word loyalty much better? That shows me that I have to pick my friends wisely. And I understand the word more, too. I hope I can find a friend like that and the friendship will last. I'm happy that my mother shared this with me. She taught me something and I hope you got something out of it, too.

TAYLUS STOREY

I chose to interview my grandmother, Ms. Elizabeth

Glasper about her personal experiences of life that help developed her character.

Back in 1936, when my grandmother was a six or seven year old child, she was already showing signs of responsibility and courage. Every morning, my grandmother's mother would set out her clothes and then, she would got to work. This continued for a while until one day on her way to school, which was a good mile away, when she left for school, the neighbors told her to hurry because there were some bad looking clouds coming. So my grandmother took their advice and sped up the pace.

When she got to school, she heard all the screams of kids and teachers. So she asked the teacher what was going on and the teacher replied, "There is a tornado coming." At that exact moment, she turned around and saw it. She said it appeared to have fire swirling in the tornado. So the teacher told the kids to go home as fast as possible. So she ran home only to find that the roof and front of her house was gone. Then she rushed to her neighbor's house and stayed with them until her mother came looking for her. And then she found her, the next two weeks, they stayed at my grandmother's mother's ex-husband's house until the Red Cross set them into an apartment. This is how my grandmother made it through the great tornado of '36.

HAI NGUYEN

"Life was hard in this place I called home. Chanh was my name, but to others here, it was worth less than the hairs on their back. My father was fighting in the war against the

VietCong. Many years passed, but a terrible thing soon occurs. My father was shot and died after. The city became too dangerous, because it had been taken over by the force of the VietCong. My husband was taken away due to his contributions to the South. Most of Vietnam was in control by the North. I had now learned the word responsibility. I had to work to support my family. Everyday, I had to go cut trees to make lumber, buy supplies, take junk from soldier's trash to sell again, and even cut trees to burn for days to make coal. I would have enough to buy my family food, get drugs for my mother, and get clothing for my family. The war grew worse, and we had to move farther to the rural areas. The war was almost at an end. My husband was released from jail. We moved from there to the United States. Here, I worked still and had a new family. I still visit Vietnam, and will always remember it."

LILIANA RIOS

Loyalty Can Change a Life

Luis and Cira meet each other at church. They exchanged phone numbers, and went out for a long time. Once they decided to stay together for the rest of their lives. They got married. They had two little kids after a long time together. They sometimes had their little discussions, but they were never more than discussions.

In the days of spring, Cira gave my brother, Luis, the surprise that she was pregnant. My brother got excited. It was not long before winter when Cira called my brother to their room.

After some time, we heard screaming, yelling, and pounding on the walls. I got really scared and went to the room. I knocked. My brother came out and went out the back door. He just said, "Everything is OK." All night, I was worried, until I fell asleep.

The next day my brother was sitting on a chair, in the dining room. I asked him if everything was alright. He answered, "She is gone forever." I asked what happened last night. I am afraid to think something bad happened to someone. He looked down and started talking. She lied all the time. She said she loved me. Everything she said was a lie. I did not understand; I asked him to explain himself. He started again. The baby she is going to have is not mine. She said that she had been with another man that was not me. She left the children with me. I asked her to leave my house. She called the man that she had been with. He came and took her with him.

After that, my brother's life has been not good at all. His kids left and have been all over everywhere. He said they talked about everything and decided they were only going to have contact because of their kids.

The kids stayed with her. My brother had a child with a woman that he was going out with. He then left her, too.

He left to go to Colorado and has not seen them. He came one month ago and saw his little girl, Angie. The little girl does not like to be with him. Maybe she does not know who we are, even though her mother tells her, and we see her every week. His two first kids came with Cira one week ago. She left them here for my brother to come and take them with him. She said that she is having problems with her husband and that she cannot have them anymore.

To this point, this has taught me that by being disloyal to the person that I have a life and a family with, is that I hurt is the person I am with, myself, and the children.

RENISE LEWIS

Respect

R- is for reliable, which my mother is

E- is for encourage because she would always have strength

S- is for school because she always accomplished her goals

P- is for patience cause she never rushed herself to nothing

E- is for emotional, because she was always on time to set her goals.

C- is for caring because she loved everybody in every way

T- is for trustworthy, because when she says she gone do something she will.

SHARI NGUYEN

Meaning of Life

When my grandpa was a young boy, he was taught about respect. In those days back then, everyone had to respect one another. When he said respect, he means answer well and with polite words. I thought it was great listening to my grandpa's life story. He told me to always respect other people everyday, no matter who or what they are. Around the house, my chore is washing the dishes. I think it's very kind to help around the house and keep it clean. Everyone has to have some kindness in them somehow. I have a friend. She is always losing something. When some of her things are gone, her mom gets really mad and starts yelling at her. She would have to go out and look for it and return it to her mom. Responsibility is when you have to take good care of your things and put them in a nice, neat place. Everyone has something to say everyday. In school, everyone needs to cooperate. If you don't have any cooperation at all, then you will lose a lot of points. You shouldn't be afraid to get it wrong because even if you do, then you just learned more. And sometimes, people just need a little patience. If you don't have patience then you are a hard person to go along with. Life is very long and if you're not patient then you are losing a lot of good things in life. When a person is not patient, then they want to get it over with really fast. But when a patient person can wait for great news, that means they don't really have to know right now, and that teaches me to wait, and I'll see.

HOPE SANDERS

I interviewed my mom on how she showed kindness.

My questions:

Q. What was the kindest thing you have ever done?

A. I took my friend's daughter to the hospital in the middle of the night because she stopped breathing.

Q. Did you feel good afterwards?

A. Yes, I felt very good afterwards.

Q. Where were you?

A. I was at home asleep.

Q. Why were you there?

A. Because I live there

Q. Who was involved?

A. Me, my friend, and her daughter

Q. When was it?

A. It was around November or December of year 2000.

Q. Why did you do it?

A. Because I have a great heart.

Q. How did you do it?

A. I got in the car and picked her up and drove her to the hospital

Q. Did you get hurt?

A. No, I did not.

Q. Were you rewarded?

A. Yes. She did not die, and they bought me a gold bracelet with hearts and crosses on it, and I felt good afterwards.

UNDRIA CLARK

Growing up in a single parent home at a very early age, he learned the meaning of responsibility by taking care of his younger sisters and brothers. The first job he ever had was at a full service gas station. He learned the meaning of cooperation from working with fellow employees. He remembers growing up as a kid entering a store and exiting the store with an item he didn't pay for, and the owner of the store caught him and took him back to his office and explained to him the meaning of integrity.

When my mother got sick, and she was confined to the bed for two months or more, the family learned the true meaning of perseverance. A few years ago, Gainesville experienced diversity when the tornado came through and destroyed schools, homes, and property.

JASPER HALE

Responsibility

My dad was in his senior year of high school when he talked my grandpa into letting him grow an afro. My grandpa told him if he did not take care of his hair, he would cut it all off. So after about eleven months, my dad stopped taking care of his hair. Then one day, my grandpa got his clippers ready for that night. My dad went to sleep and that night my grandpa went into his room and cut off all his hair. That morning, my dad looked on the floor and saw his hair. And that's the year my dad lost his afro.

ESMERALDA AGUIRRE

Interview with my mom
Responsibility!!!

When my mom was thirteen,
My mom had her room by herself now
Now she was old enough now she was a teen

She had to keep it pretty and clean
She had to wash her stuff and sometimes make her stuff.
She also had to keep up with her stuff
So that's how my mom learned responsibility.

LYNDSAY MERCER

Patience!

Mom: Elizabeth, put your brother's shoes on.

Liz: Why? Mom, he never lets me.

Mom: Do it now.

Liz: Fine (shy)...Come here, Robby.

Robby: (sits down)

Liz: Give me your foot.

Robby: Why do you have to be so mean?

Liz: I'm not...Stop curling up your toes. I can't put your shoes on.

Narrator: After putting on Robby's shoes until he learned himself, Elizabeth learned how to use patience.

GRICELDA MIRANDA

Well, my cousin said that he always respected the people older than him. He told me that he had to have cooperation at work with everybody. And he chose patience because he always waited and waited until it was his turn. And he chose kindness too because he had to be kind to everybody; if not, he got in trouble. And he chose responsibility too because he needed to go at the exact time to work and take whatever he needed to take to work. And to not forget anything, and he always went to work. And that is my cousin's life when he started to grow up.

LIZZ OVERDORFF

Responsibility

About 40 years ago, my father stopped getting an allowance. He had to get a job as a paperboy at the age of twelve. He had to learn to be responsible. He was even fussed out so much that he never delivered that lady a paper again. That was one of the longest jobs he ever had. He only made $.07 per paper, but that was a lot back then.

MARIA RAMIREZ

Interview with my grandpa

When my grandfather was little, he learned his lesson about respect. He was about 12 years old, and he wanted to get a job. He was walking from school when a man came in his truck and asked him something. He did not respond, and that did not show respect. When he got home, his dad took him to find a job. It just happened that the owner was the same man. So he scared my grandfather. When he told him he was not going to give him a job, my grandfather got sad. He didn't want to go anywhere. One day, the old man came to his house and told him he needed help at the factory. He asked him if he wanted to help him. Of course, he said yes. When my grandfather's father found out, he gave my grandfather a spanking. From that day on, he learned that he had to respect his elders.

NIUJING JIANG

Responsibility

When my mom was 15 years old, her mom told her to bring some papers to the place she worked. My mom forgot to do that because she was playing with her friends. After she went home, her mom was very mad at her because she didn't bring the papers. The papers were very important to her job. My mom learned that she had to be more responsible and remember what she needed to do.

RANDY TRAN

Interview

Once my parents lived in Vietnam, and they weren't so rich. My dad was working at the dock, and my mom was cooking and taking care of my brother. My dad was fishing for dinner everyday before he came home from work. My dad had to go to war, so things weren't so great. My parents argued most of the time. My parents had enough money to go to California then they lived there for twelve years. They got bored of California, so they decided to move to Georgia. My dad said that they would never argue again because it doesn't mean anything or you don't get anything when you argue.

LATIFAH STRICKLAND

Responsibility

When my mother was a teenager, she had to learn responsibility. She had to budget her time between work and school. She managed to do it, so she could buy things like personal stuff, school clothes, and school stuff. When her mother was in a tight, she would help her. She is also my grandmother.

What responsibility is all about is a person's word. Never say you are going to do something and never do it. That's not called responsibility. My mother said it was hard to work and go to school.

She managed it, though. She graduated from high school and went on to college.

JEROMY YARBROUGH

Personal Experiences

I asked my dad (Jerome Yarbrough) to do an interview about the following subjects: Respect, cooperation, loyalty, responsibility, and patience. He responded with the following answers:

Respect is something you have to earn in life; it all starts with giving respect to your parents and any adults you cross in life. Respect was always a part of my childhood; I knew nothing else. It was a part of life.

Cooperation is something you will have to have to make it in today's world. I tried to do things alone, and it was very hard, but with cooperation with others, it made life simple.

Courage is something we all have, but it takes some pushing to get it out of some people. Being in the U.S. Army gave me a lot of courage to be a leader and not a follower.

By being a member of the fire department and helping others, it requires me to be responsible and loyal and have patience and stay calm so I can perform at my best.

ANA CRUZ

Lonely all alone
No one to talk to
I feel all lonely
Tied up in a tree
Just because I did not
Want to go to school
That's how I learned to
Be responsible

My mom did not want to go to school. What my grandmother did was to tie up my mom to a tree almost all day until school ended.

CINDY DELGADO

In 1970, a young girl was about twelve years old. One day, one of her neighbors asked her if she could do her a favor. And the young Janice said, "Yes, I will."

Her neighbor told her she was going to Canada for a while. And she left Janice with some big responsibilities. One she had was to feed her two cats. Two, she had to water her garden of flowers. Three, she had to take out all the vegetables from the vegetable garden.

She had to do all those chores everyday. And you know her neighbor really trusted her. Her neighbor even left her the key to the house. She really trusted Janice because her neighbor knows her very well because her neighbor was her third grade teacher.

She paid Janice two dollars a day. And Janice never did anything wrong. She turned out to be very responsible. When her neighbor came back from Canada, she brought her back a very beautiful China plate and another gift.

Janice Bowen now today is forty-five and very, very responsible.

ALBERTO RUIZ

My mom taught me the word responsibility from doing my chores. She would take something I like if I didn't do my chores. Now I'm in the habit of doing my chores, so that word I learned from my mom and chores.

KELSEY MAINE

Responsibility
When my dad was a kid, he had gerbils. He had to clean them regularly. He also had to clean their cages. He had to feed them everyday. He also had to take them to the vet to keep them healthy. If he failed those responsibilities, they would get sick or die.

BRENNEN OWENS

Responsibility
Once when my mom was 10 years old, she got her first puppy named Bear. She said that she took good care of him. She fed him four times a day. And she walked him four miles everyday.

She said she learned a lot of responsibility. She said she was glad that she got the dog. And it taught her a lot. And that is my story on responsibility.

D.J. MCDUFFIE

Patience
1 child, 2 children, 3 children, 4
5 children, 6 children, 7 children
no more
That's how many children my grandma had
One of them married the man I called dad
That's how she learned her lesson of patience
With all those children, I wonder how she made it
I know it was hard but she prevailed over it all
She made it through but not all on one shoe
Not with Church's chicken but by asking spicy or mild
1 child, 2 children, 3 children, 4
5 children, 6 children, 7 children
No more

LACEY WALLINGFORD

The Sinking Bus
(using the tune of the Brady Bunch)

This is a story of a youth group sinking.
One their way to Minnesota.
As they crossed over a roadway,
They skidded and fell all the way down.
The sinking bus,
The sinking but,

That's the way they all learned courage.

The song above is about when my mom was in a bus accident on a youth retreat to go camping in Minnesota. They crossed over a bridge and skidded and plunged into the water below. That's how they learned courage.

LIDUVINA LEON

My Grandfather's Lesson

When my grandfather, Jose, was a little boy, his father made sure he learned a lesson about responsibility. His father had given him some money to hold for him. That money was going to go to the savings the family had. I am not sure how much it was, but it was a lot back in his days. After he had given the money to him, his friend came. His friend, Rodrigo, had some beautiful marbles. My grandfather thought they were cool! My grandfather and Rodrigo came to a deal. He gave the money to Rodrigo. When my grandfather's dad found out, he was furious! They talked to Rodrigo's dad, and everything was OK. After that, my grandfather had a lot of responsibilities to do at home. He did learn his lesson!!

JORDAN STANLEY

It was the year 1981. I was 15 years old and had just started driving. My parents were out of town on vacation, and the babysitter was at her work picking up something. She said she'd be right back. So I decided to drive my dad's company car around the neighborhood. After a couple of times around, I noticed a neighbor staring at me. After a while I started to watch the neighbor instead of the road and ran over some mailboxes, which damaged the hood of the company car. After I realized what I had done, I also realized I had to tell my parents what I had done. That night when they called, I worked up enough courage to tell them. When my parents got back, part of my punishment was to take responsibility for the accident, and they made me write a letter of apology to my dad's boss explaining how I took the car without permission and got into an accident. My dad's boss was not expecting a letter from me. He realized how hard and how much courage it took for me to write the letter, so he told my dad the company would take care of the damage. The bottom line is this: I learned no matter how hard it is to take full responsibility for my actions, I have to have courage to do so because you never know when the outcome will be a positive one.

ELVA AND JANETH ESCALERA

Responsibility: Roger

When Roger was 20 years old, he got shot. He lost 7 pints of blood. They put back 10 pints of blood.

He was up to 3 days in the hospital. That was lucky for him to live. Roger's mother stayed with him day and night and prayed for him to get better. One day the doctors said, "Roger, you would not be able to walk no more, and this will be hard to accept."

Roger stayed in the hospital 9 months. He stayed flat on his flat back in bed.

Now this is a true story. "I am living right now because my mother prayed for me and God was with me all times. If my mother didn't pray, I might not be living, but I am living."

If you don't believe it, come to "Good News at Noon" and ask for Roger.

Today, I decided to live with God. Being with God changed my life forever.

"I owe this life to God."

SELVI ORTIZ

Responsibility
I have a friend
She is a great
Friend,
But she said
A story
A story
About responsibility
She said she had
A baby
A baby when
She was 21,
She knew she
Had responsibility

To take care
Of her baby,
She said, you
Never know
And you
May never
Will
But she said
That's how
She knows about
Responsibility!

CHRISTIAN SUMMEROUR

My grandmother and I are really close. I see her at least once every two months. She lives in Nashville, TN. She has a big, blue house. She has 6 children that are grown-up. Me and my grandma talked about responsibility, respect, kindness, and cooperation.

When my grandmother was a little girl, she had to learn her timetables, just as we have today. One day, when she came home from school, her dad told her to learn the timetables from 1-5. The next day, when her dad came home, she didn't know her timetables. She tried to hide behind her grandfather. Her dad told her that it was her responsibility to learn her timetables. If she didn't know her timetables the next day, she was going to be in serious trouble. Guess what? My grandmother learned her timetables in two days.

My grandmother had several chores that she had to do every-day. It was her responsibility to fill and bring a water bucket inside after she arrived home from school.

My older sister would do her homework everyday when she would get out of school. She always told me to get my home-work. As I grew older, it was the first thing I would do when I arrived from school. I respected my sister for teaching me to complete my homework before I went to play.

My mother died when I was very young, and it was hard being without her. I had one friend named Kathy that would come everyday. She would come over some days and just sit. We never said a word. This was a friend that came over and showed true kindness until I was able to play and be happy.

ANGEL SHIELDS

Roses are red, violets are blue. Sugar is sweet and so are you. Geneva is the sweetest mother I ever had in my life, and my sister Eleanor is sweet too, but I love both of my families. My other mother, Debbie Williams died before I went to New York for our family reunion. We stayed for three days. Then we went home. I started school when I was in the fourth grade. I would get in trouble all the time, but my mother Geneva Shields talked to me and encouraged me to do good in school. On the last day of school, she passed away, and that made me very sad. I will always remember the things that she taught me, and I will try really hard to do things the way she taught me.

RENEE CROCE

This is the biography of Alan Croce.
These events happened 40-45 years ago.

Alan's Story:

Alan Croce had light brown hair, brown eyes, and olive skin. Alan was 12 years old when he went to a car realtor with his grandfather in Brooklyn, New York.

See, the salesman was a fast-talking, greedy, slick man. The salesman wanted to charge Alan and his grandfather $2,600 for the car that they wanted to buy, but Alan's friend's parents bought the same exact car for $2,200. Alan knew that his grandfather was being overcharged. "Let's go grandpa," Alan said glumly. As Alan and his grandfather turned to leave, the greedy salesman ran into the parking lot and virtually came into the car. "Hold on," the salesman pleaded to his customers, "I'll give the car to you for $2,100." "Wow, was that a good deal!" Alan thought to himself. He turned to his grandfather and said reassuringly, "Buy it!"

The next day, Alan Croce's grandfather was bragging about the price of his new car and raving over "Alan my boy."

As Alan got older, in the summer of his junior year, he got a job at his high school as a custodian. It was a very responsible job, I must tell you. Alan had to be there on time at 8AM to 4PM. He also learned how to operate power tools safely.

When Alan Croce was 17, he was on a semi-pro baseball team. Alan knew that he had to cooperate with his coach, people who were as good as he or better, and to cooperate with his team-mates who were 20 or 30 years old.

In baseball and football, the young man knew that he was good. He persevered to accomplish his dream, which was to become a major league baseball player. He would go over to his friend's house every day in the summer and play stickball to prac-tice for the new season. (Just a note: As you can see, Alan was geared a lot towards sports.)

When Alan was 17, a lot of events in his life happened. Another event was this: On November 1963, an awful event hap-pened. President John F. Kennedy was assassinated. President Kennedy's death taught Alan and his friends that life was very precious and a person as great as President Kennedy in a blink of an eye was gone. Alan and his peers thought the president's death was inconceivable.

Soon after, Alan graduated from Hewlett High School.

CAROLINA SANABRIA

You should respect everyone around you,
I'll give you a clue.
You should respect your parents,
As you should your grandparents.
You should respect your elders,
As you should respect the yellers.
You should respect your dad,
As you should that lad.
You should respect your mom,

As you should respect Tom.
If you don't respect your teachers,
They won't give you good grades neither.
Respect everyone.

When my mom was in high school (1985), there was an earthquake in Mexico City. My mom's group asked for the teachers to give them the day off. They went downtown to collect money to send over to the people that needed it. The money that was collected was given to the Red Cross. This demonstrates kindness and cooperation.

My grandma taught my mom to respect everyone and everyone's way of thinking, to respect her parents, to respect her family, and her friends. She thinks that by respecting life and people's decisions, you can keep the family together and friends forever.

In Durango, there is a fair every year to celebrate the foundation of the city. You can find a diversity of crafts and foods from different cultures and different people.

My mom had a friend that drank too much. And it was something hard for his family and friends. But they all had patience for him and gave him advice and talked to him and finally after a long time, he gave up drinking. We all had patience, and he did it.

When my mom started to work at her job, her job was heavy and dirty. But she would stay overtime when they asked her to. And she had other jobs her supervisor asked her to do. She did her jobs well. Now she is only in charge of the chemicals, and it's an easier job, and she gets paid better.

JOYCE CLARK

Short scene:

Me: Can you think of a story from when you were younger
that taught you the meaning of one of these words?

Interviewer: My name is Donna Clark. I'll use the word
respect because as a child, your neighbor was just like
your parent if you did something wrong and your parent
wasn't around, they was just like your parent and you
gave them respect.

Me: Did you have a job or responsibility that taught you
about 1 of the words?

Interviewer: Well, when I was growing up, I didn't have a
job. The only responsibility I had was to go to school and
make good passing grades.

Me: Did another person help you understand 1 of these
words?

Interviewer: Well, yes. My mother taught me the meaning of
the word responsibility because every time she would go
to work she would leave me in the house with my
brothers and my next door neighbor would come over
and watch us.

Me: Can you think of a difficult situation that helped you
understand 1 of these words?

Interviewer: I can't remember if someone did, but I can say I
didn't understand the word courage until I had my own f
family.

Me: Can you think of an event in your community that
taught you or another young

person a lesson about life?

Interviewer: Look both ways before you cross the street because something happened to a girl we knew. She was getting off the Marta bus to use the phone to tell her mother that she was on her way home. She ran across the street, and as she was running, she was not paying attention. She saw her friends running, so she ran and got hit by the same Marta bus she had just gotten off of.

JACQUIESE WHELCHEL

My mom and her sisters used to get along with each other. They used to play softball and volleyball together. They didn't have much back then.

ALI ARROYO

What I am writing about is from my mom when she was my age. Over there in Mexico, she had to ride one of those smelly and old buses. Whenever it was the weekdays, my mom had to stay at a different house. Everyday after she came back from school, she went to that house. While she was there, she did her homework. After she was done with her homework, she went with her friends to play some hoops. The sad part of all of this is that she could only see her mom on the weekend. While there, she did her homework. Also, she helped her mom with the work she had to do.

JUAN GARCIA

My grandmother is 63 years old. She went to the second grade only. In her times, there were not a lot of cars and not even pavement road. She came to America to see her children that are adults. She had 12 children and 2 died at the age of 2 months. In school, their parents had to bring their lunch to eat.

BREANNA BRYANT

When I was young, it was different than it is today. We did not have microwaves or any other nice advantages. They came out in the 1960's. I went to White Sulfer when I was in kindergarten through sixth grade. When I was in the seventh grade, I was in the high school. I had to be on the bottom locker. The seniors would drop books on your head. I liked high school even though there was a guy that made fun of my glasses. One day he got his eyes stuck cross-eyed from making fun of me. I had long black hair all the way down my back. I remember going to the racetrack. I won a lot of races. I got my own racecar in high school. When I was a senior, I was on top locker, so I got to drop books on top of the freshmen. I remember the feeling of the racecar. I graduated a senior.

JULIE PARKS

This is an example of diversity. This story is about my

mom. She is 55 years old, and her name is Clarice Parks. This story takes place back when she was my age. When she was in school, about middle school, they had a school for the white kids and a school for the black kids. She went through childhood only being friends with white kids because back then it was wrong to be seen with different colored friends. Then when she went to high school, it all changed because that was the start of black and white schools. She went half-way through the school year not talking to a black kid 'cause it was wrong, or so she thought. Then one day, she got a project to work with a partner, and that was the first day she ever talked to a black person. They worked on the project for a week. Then they became friends. She started hanging out with her everyday after and in school. When her white friends saw her, they didn't want to be seen with her because of her new friends. And all the black kids didn't want to be friends with her because she was white. When she grew up, she was glad that when there was racism that she had one true friend, and she was proud of her friend's color.

NANCY ACOSTA

Catalina Garcia was born in 1925, raised by both parents in a town called Rio Verde, San Luis in Mexico. She dropped out of school at age twelve when she was about to finish sixth grade. The reason was because she had to help her mom with the chores. She had six brothers and two sisters. She was the oldest one. A big responsibility for her was that she had to take care of all of them while her mom and dad were working. Then Catalina got married when she was eighteen. She married a man named Alquilino. They had five sons and one daughter. Her name is Guadalupe. Her husband died when she was sixty-eight years old. Since he died, Catalina's life changed. She's single right now. She's seventy-eight years old. She comes to visit her daughter Guadalupe here in Georgia but still lives in the "old town" as she calls it to live with her youngest son Luis.

DARIUS WILKINS

I started school at Northwestern Elementary School in nineteen forty-eight. Schools were a lot different then. I only went to school with other black children. We had all black teachers.

Our teachers demanded a great deal of respect. Parents were very supportive of the teachers. If a student got in trouble at school, he was in trouble at home. The teachers would personally walk you home to make sure your parents knew that you were in trouble.

Teachers encouraged us to do our best, often staying after school or coming to our homes to help us with homework that was hard for us.

We were a big community of people working together, encouraging each other on a daily basis. It was hard, and we had to get along.

Schoolrooms were often crowded and hot in summer, cold in winter. We were responsible for bringing in firewood or cleaning blackboards and sometimes the lunchroom. We had to work really hard, but it taught us responsibility.

T.J. BENNETT

My History

My name is Claudine Grindle Moore. I was born on April 17, 1950 in Gainesville, Georgia. I was the eighth child born; I had four sisters and five brothers, one of which is my twin. All of my brothers and sisters were born at home, but me and my twin brother, Claude, were the first born in a hospital. I learned responsibility in my life and respect.

I attended Gainesville Mill for first through fourth grade, I attended Miller Park for fifth through sixth grade. I attended Gainesville Middle School for seventh through eighth grade, and I attended Gainesville High School for ninth through tenth grade. After tenth grade, I quit school. I dropped out because I got married to a young man named Billy Moore. I had a child at seventeen, which was my daughter, Sharon.

I got my first job at a chicken plant when I was sixteen years old. I got my first long-term job at an assembly plant, Potter and Brumfield. I worked there for fourteen years. I had some odd jobs in between, and then I got a job with ZF Industries, which is where I have been working for the past fifteen years.

I went to a school that had blacks and whites separated. I only liked school when I was going through grade school. When I got to Gainesville High School, blacks and whites were no longer separated. That is when school wasn't all that fun anymore. I did not like it because I always was the last one. Kids would make fun of me, pick on me, and so many other things.

When I went back to school to get my high school diploma, it was more fun. I think that it was more fun because people respected me better. At twenty-one, I had my second child, which was my son Jeff.

I sang on the radio when I was a little girl at age twelve. I got my first TV when I was nine years old in 1959. I had a grandson before I was forty, and his name was T.J. I saw Elvis at a concert at age twenty-three in 1973. When I was a little girl, I used an outhouse. I did not have indoor plumbing until I was nine years old.

My husband died October 1, 2000, at the age of fifty-two; I was fifty years old.

JONAS JENKINS

My story is about my 97 year old grandmother Cassie Jeraldine Tabor

In my lifetime, we were taught responsibility and respect. I had to watch my brothers and sisters while my parents worked in the cotton fields. We weren't outside playing and playing video games. We had to work inside the house, cleaning, doing laundry, or other household chores.

I remember times we had to walk miles to school on dirt roads, no bus, going places and being turned around because of the color of your skin by the white storekeepers. If there were signs up with whites only, black people were not allowed in.

I married at the age of 12 in a little shack which was the courthouse by a judge. I had my first child at 13. I only went to the third grade in school. I had 13 children and all of them were born at home. Six out of thirteen of the kids are deceased, a set of triplets Lola Mae, Ola Jay and Carter K, a set of twins, Eddie and Eddie Sue, and another son, Felton, who died 2 years ago. My children, which are still living is Cassie (the oldest and first born), Carrie, Fannie Sue, Margaret, J.D., Waymon, and Jessie.

In my lifetime, there was diversity and segregation among blacks and whites. It took a lot of prayer, patience, and courage back then. I say this because of the way black people were treated all because of the color of our skin. I remember walking through crowds, being spit on (in the face), having things thrown at you, and being called all kinds of names.

In spite of it all, my parents taught us to love regardless of the color of a person's skin. My mother would always tell me to pray for the people who mistreated me.

I am old in age, and I live alone since my husband died twenty-two years ago. I am in my right mind, though my memory gets short at times. I am thankful for the years added on to my life. My mother lived to be 105, and I pray I will be around just as long.

NUVIA VELASQUEZ

I learned that respect is the best thing. We had to be respectful because you have to respect the teachers and parents and uncle and aunts. You feel good if you respect the other persons. If you don't respect the other persons, you feel bad. My mom said that being respectful is the nice thing because the people said that girl is so respectful, and they feel good if you are respectful to the other people. Then your mom feels wonderful about you, and you feel great about yourself.

ACENCION MOLINA

There was one word that changed my life, responsibility. This word is thought to be everything in life. When I was little, about your age, I didn't like to go to school, but some days I loved school. But I had to work in the farmlands cause when I was little, I didn't have what you have or what you can accomplish just by listening and paying attention in class. I didn't get that will and now you see me where I'm working at. When I was little, my biggest responsibilities were to help my dad out working and going to school. Time passed, and I couldn't handle them anymore both, at the same time. Sometimes I missed school, and others I didn't. We needed something, but without the money, we couldn't buy it. So one day, I had to choose one of two things: The work that was hard and difficult or the school where I just sat to learn new things. I wanted to choose the school, but we needed money. So I had to work hard to help my dad out with the money till I raised enough money to come over here and start working with the half or none of the money I got cause the other half or sometimes all I give it to my dad for the things we needed. My two greatest responsibilities I had and have are you and your sister.

KORTNEY WHITE

Yes I (Michael Waller) went to Gainesville Middle School way back in the 70's. Back then, blacks and whites had just started going to school together. Integration was also just starting, so there were no Hispanics or Vietnamese. Since integration was just starting, there were some who were still prejudiced. It was hard on them teachers and us students. Well child, I remember this one time, let me see, it was the first day of my 7th grade year. My mother had given me a homemade sweater to wear. I was kind of ashamed of it. But anyway, this young white fellow comes up to me and says move and pushes me. Now I ain't the type to start things, but he was pushing it. So the next thing I know, the principal was pulling me off of the boy. Now of course he lied and said I started it. That little fight taught all a big lesson. The only way to stay out of trouble is to respect the rules and then cooperate with them.

DOMINIQUE WOODS

Annette Woods was 13 years old and attended Alcorn Middle School in the year of 1978. Two years before, she and her family moved from Elgin Air Force Base in Florida, to Ridgewood in Columbia, South Carolina. That same year, she moved across town to Green Oaks. Even though she went to the same school, her friends changed. She became friends with the people in the neighborhood. She and her family found a place in the new community.

When they moved to Green Oaks from Ridgewood, they saw a big difference in the community. The Ridgewood community was made up of mainly whites and not a lot of youths. Green Oaks was made up of mainly blacks and with a lot more youths. Ridgewood's parents were older, while Green Oaks' parents were younger. When asked, "How did these moves teach you the importance of some of the character education words given?" Annette said that she learned to respect and to have responsibility. Every move they made, she had to make sure she woke up on time for school, ate breakfast, and caught the bus. If she had not, she would have had to skip school that day. Her mom could not take her because she did not have a car and caught the city bus to work before her children woke up. If Annette missed too many days of school, she would have failed the eighth grade

She also had to respect people in the community and at school. There were different diversities, and she had to respect the fact that they were all different, and she had to respect their customs. She probably would not have made friends if she did not do that. She could have gotten beat up. That year, Annette learned that she could get along with many different types of people. She is a people person.

Annette Woods learned about respect and responsibility by her family moving. Making friends and accepting that everyone was different took a lot of respect. Responsibility came with having to wake up in the mornings and those such things. Without responsibility, Annette would have graduated a year later than her classmates, maybe even two years if she had not learned to be responsible. These are only two of many other words that are important in life. It is never too early to learn the character education words.

VANESSA RAMIREZ

I asked my dad if Gainesville has changed. He said for the 15 years he has been in Gainesville, the answer was yes. He said Gainesville was smaller. More people are living here now. More houses and factories are being made. The factories were smaller than now. Our factories right now are bigger. We got over 300 people in each factory. They are starting to get more working places too! He says the population of people are growing each month.

BRENTARA RUCKER

I am doing respect. When my moma was growing up, she could not leave or go anywhere without an adult. She showed so much respect that she never got in trouble. Until one day, she snuck out of the house without any adult. So that night when she got home, her parents were waiting on her. Then they asked, "Where have you been?" and she said I am sorry that I didn't show any respect. Now she has learned that she needs to show respect to get the respect back. She has taught her kids to show respect if you want it back. So now we have learned you got to show respect to get respect.

ELIZABETH MOORE

I'm writing a story about my stepfather, Joe. He was in the Army, and his job was to jump out of airplanes. He had to be very courageous to do the things he did. When he jumped out of the planes, he carried over 100 pounds and was 800 feet in the air. He jumped out of airplanes over 100 times.

After he was in the Army 10 years, he went to Ranger School. It was and still is the hardest school to complete and/or be in, in the United States.

When it was time to join, there were 392 people who tried to be a Ranger; but knowing how hard it is, not even half of them made it to graduation. Guess how many graduated? 92! Hardly anyone made it. But Joe did, and guess what? He was first in the class. After only 92 made it and 392 entered, and he made the best one, he must have worked hard.

SHERRNACE BONDS

Positive Character Trait

One day my mom and dad told me a story about when they were little. It was about when they were in high school and when they grew up together. My mom's name was Sherry, and my dad's name was Darryl. They were in different classes. My mom was in the 9th grade, and so was my dad. They went to Gainesville High School or a different school. My mom and dad had a lot of friends back then. My mom used to hang out with my aunts, her sisters, her brothers, and some boys and girls, when she was young. My dad used to hang out with his sisters, his brothers, his uncles, some boys and girls. They used to have fun. When they were getting older, they kept on getting good grades. When they were in college, they got their degree. Now they want me to get my degree.

NAYELI NUNEZ

Respect

Once upon a time, there was a girl who lived in a place where they sell drugs. She knew it was not a good place to live. She had lots of friends, though. She loved to hang around with them. We always had things to cheer everybody up when they were sad.

Her mom always said to behave and respect my friends, and they'll respect me. Until one day, she fell in love with one of her friends. She thought he was cute. But she knew that her mom would not accept her friend.

One day, she told her mom she was going for a walk. She went for a walk with the boy she loved. After that, her mom was unhappy with her. Everyone started talking about things that weren't true. She learned not everybody is going to respect you until you respect them.

JOHNNY MILLSAP

When I was 8 years old, I had a hamster named

Chomper. When Chomper died, I buried him in my backyard. That day, I cried and I cried, and my dad said, "Your hamster died because you didn't show responsibility to him."

So my dad took me to the pet store so I can get a hamster. We bought a hamster named Clover. Clover was the best hamster ever, and I showed responsibility by loving her, feeding her, cleaning her cage, and taking care of her.

The next day, my friend Justin came over with Cinastick, and while me and Justin were watching TV, Cinastick and Clover had babies. I let Justin take two home, and I kept three. I named them Cinastick, Jr., Cinamina and Mila.

And when Justin ever came over, he would bring Monica, Smokey, and Tina. Justin would put the three hamsters in the cage and Cinastick too, and they would play together. Plus, we would put tubs in the cage, and they would chew it up like a rabbit. Me and Justin laughed and laughed. Then Justin's mother called, and Justin would have to go home. That day, I learned responsibility and respect, and I hope you will, too.

GREGORY STENZEL

Courage

When my father was five years old, there was a really huge tornado watch. My grandpa had a bad broken leg. As they were watching the weather channel, the front door ripped off the house, and my father had to be very brave and carry his baby sister down the pitch-black stairs.

JALEESA SMITH

Perseverance as told by Kerry Moore

When I was a young child, my mother was very ill and hospitalized for a very long time. Perseverance was something I learned to understand during this time. Not knowing what perseverance meant, my father taught me the patient effort of remaining positive during this time. So perseverance became a continued effort during my mother's four year battle with cancer. Having perseverance during this time helped me remain steadfast and focused during each day that passed. After my mother's inability to beat the cancer passed, perseverance became even more important for me on a daily basis to continue on with my daily focus while recovering from the loss of my mother.

KELLY MATTICK

The Big Game of 1936

In 1936, my Aunt Johanna was in her senior year at Plains High in Pennsylvania. Girls' sports were not as popular or as abundant as today. Winning this championship was a big boost to girls' sports at her school.

I walked out onto the court. I remembered being nervous on my first basketball game. My fiend, Babe, was just as nervous as I. We stepped into the bright light to shouts, claps and a banner that had "Go Plains High" on it. As our team jogged out and we got set up, our coach was saying he was proud. The ball was thrown upwards. Our team got it; we scored.

In the fourth quarter the score was tied. There was one minute left. Our team had the ball. Pass after pass went up the court. Ten seconds left on the clock and with one great pass to Babe, she put it in. The buzzer went off. We had the championship in the bag!

Afterwards we had a party in the gym. Our coach talked about all the cooperation that had been needed to get to this championship. Yes, as I thought about it, we had all worked so well together. We had become more than just a team. We had become friends off the court also. It's something I have always remembered, you can accomplish a lot when you have cooperation.

JIMENA AYALA

Gracias por su atencion

A mother holds her children's hands for just a little while, but she holds their hearts forever.

En los anos de mi infonsia Yo hera muy feliz en Mexico me divertia con mis amigos y cuando y ba a la escuela.

Pero en el ano 2000, me vine a conocer los estados unidos y me paresia un estado muy maravillos a que yo e cumplido mis megores suenos del mundo e conocido mucha gente diferente aunque extrano mi familia pero hace 4 anos que no e vuelto a hir para haya creo que mean pasado muchas cosas como agur a prendi hacer un buen decorador de areglos y tantas cosas mas porgue en Mexico nunca lo hice y a qui aprendi a manegar y a hora tengo mi carro y hacy aprendi a valorar mis cosas y las de las damas personas bueno eso es una parte de mi Historia.

Gracias

KHADIJAH ALI

Interview with Shannon Ali

As a young girl, when my mama was in high school, she saw a lot of girls getting pregnant. She saw the responsibility of having a baby. She would watch her friends take care of their babies by changing diapers and feeding them. When she got married, she had a baby girl named Khadijah Imane Ali. She had the same responsibility as the other girls. Her chores were to take care of her newborn baby and put clothes on the baby's back. When her mom got sick, she was in a coma for a month, so she couldn't walk or talk. She had to learn how to do those things all over again. She was patient. One day, they got a phone call that her cousin was in a car wreck and was killed. It was very sad because it was her cousin and they were very close, like brother and sister.

ALAN GARCIA

My mom helped her mom by cleaning up the house. My mom took care of her brothers and sisters. She fed their pets.

When she was around 8 years old, she had to be responsible for washing her own clothes. She was responsible for her own things.

Her mom showed her how to respect her older family and other people.

My mom was patient with her brother. When she was in a store to buy things, she had to be patient because of a line. She had to be patient in school, waiting until she went inside her school each morning.

BIANCA SERNA

Responsibility

My best friend Rosio told me something about responsibility. When she was little, she had lots of responsibilities. But one of the most important responsibilities of all her life was having to take care of her mom and dad. They were very sick, and she was always there for them as her parents. She had to give them medicine, give them food, and love them even if they were sick. All that happened when she was 17, and they felt better when she was 20. She had to be with them 4 years. She said that she didn't care how many years she didn't have fun or go out with friends. The important thing was that she was able to help her parents feel much better, and that was a big responsibility for her. But the important thing was that her parents were OK. Of all this, she learned new things, like she didn't know at first what she was going to do with the responsibility. She learned that it's not easy at first. But, then you get used to it.

MONTERIAZ RILEY

I will be interviewing my grandmother. The character trait she shows is responsibility. "I have always been the kind of person that liked to keep my house clean. We were given different chores on a daily basis. As I grew older, the chores were not enough. I wanted more things to do, so I begged my mom to let me go to other area homes and work to make money! I would work every weekend and made extra money. I was taught how to budget my money. My workload increased to other jobs. Working at an early age has taught me a greater sense of financial responsibility. My goal in life is to be out of debt. I've already claimed it." I could learn responsibility because she teaches me a lot of it, and I think she is a great person.

SONIA ZAVALA

Sandra, my sister, was so irresponsible. She had to show responsibility to my mother and father. One day, Sandra said, "I know I can be responsible, so what can I do to show my mom and dad?" Sandra got this idea that she will take care of her smaller sister and brother. That is me and my brother, Jr. Sandra told my mom and dad about it, and they weren't really sure, but then they agreed so that taking care of us would make Sandra responsible. She wasn't really our guardian. My aunt lived next door, and she was checking on us all the time, and sometimes, we spent the night at her house. Sandra was taking this serious. She was after us a lot, especially Jr., who is a troublemaker. Now Sandra was growing responsible. My mother and father were seeing that and decided to raise her allowance. Sandra has become responsible a whole lot more than she used to be.

ERICA FREEZE

My Mom:

I lost my dad at a very young age. So did my mom and my brother and sister. It was a very great loss. My mom had to take care of us so young and by herself. She is a responsible, independent woman and mother. She always listened to us when we had to tell her something. She was always there when we needed her. Then, she got married to my step-dad. But we were number one in her life. She took care of us when we were young. She still takes care of us, and she is the number one mom in my book. That's the story about my mom. I love her so much. I hope all of ya'll love your mom like I do. Because she was like a dad, and she was the mom!

ANGELA WANG

Responsibility

My sister was a Junior Staff at Camp Dove last spring. Her name is Helen. She's 16 years old, and her job was too overwhelming. Helen had to watch over kids and had to stay up very late, plus she had to wake up early. Before the kids came, she thought she could handle it. The kids, she thought, would be a piece of cake. Oh boy, was Helen wrong! Helen said that this wasn't an easy job at all, and she realized that she had to take a lot of responsibility for the kids. Then the kids came, and I came to greet them, too. Since the first day of camp, many kids have fun times and meet many new faces. A couple of hours later, some kids were out of control and didn't pay any attention to their counselors! I saw their counselors tried to stop them. We had different color groups, and then a young boy was in Helens's group. A boy was OUT OF CONTROL and ignored Helen. She had a hard time to get him back in the group, but all of a sudden, he started to run away from my sister. Helen was responsible for that boy. I saw my sister started to run after him, and I was like, "Wow, my sister doesn't have a lot of strength to run after that boy!" Then finally, she caught him! I could see that Helen was so tired to catch him. Helen told me that her body was so achy because of that boy! After that, she was so tired and felt like she took care of kids in the zoo! Since the last day of camp... many kids went home and my sister was so exhausted. My sister and I went home from the camp. I saw my sister was like a zombie. I know my sister had been working so hard since the first day of camp. I know how she felt, and it was a lot of responsibility taking care of the kids. Next time, you think it's going to be easy, but THINK AGAIN!

ARYIAN GWIN

My word is respect. My dad didn't learn respect. It was just something he was told. That is what he told me. You have to learn respect before you can have it. My mom and dad have had respect since they were little kids. Respect is a very, very important thing to learn. If you do not know or learn what respect is, you could be hurt or disciplined. Learning or being taught respect is something that you and everyone else should learn. I know what respect is. Respect is having honor for an older person, which is an example. Another example of having respect is calling an older person yes ma'am, no ma'am, yes sir, and no sir.

JAMEISHA WRIGHT

Kindness
Kindness means to be kind
Kind
In love
Nice to others
Don't be mean
Never talk about others
Everybody has to be nice
Sweet
So nice to others and yourself

Show kindness to everyone and they'll be kind and have some fun. Being kind is the thing to do. Showing kindness is the thing for you.

CHRIS RUCKER

He always made messes with his brothers, and when his mama got home, she always had to clean up after them. Then one day, he saw her cleaning up and that disheartened him, and from then on, he has helped people who needed help. That event has encouraged him to help people who try to do positive things for themselves.

My Aunt and My Mama

My mama had to teach my aunt Trice to sing for a singing contest a long time ago. My mama wanted to show responsibility, so she kept up on her sister's lessons. When the day of the singing contest came, my aunt sung and won the contest. Now, the trophy is in the trophy case in the house.

JOSHUA CHESTER

Patience Poem
Patience, a virtue my mother did learn
While waiting some years for her own turn.
It all started 'bout 1967,
A sophomore in high school in a class of eleven.
While belonging to the band,
A clarinet was finally thrust in her hand.
Lloyd Tarpley, that was his name,
Patience, to my mother, he helped explain.
She accepted this not ignoring
So that her music would not be boring.

Mountain View High School, on mount up to high,
Her memories of there are ever so high.
She thinks no different of it now,
The opportunity was great,
Though now you ask, "How?"
In raising her children patience has played a role
For some of those times that are awfully slow.
The future, she believes,
Her outlook will not change at all,
She will believe this doth the roof fall.
So, in conclusion, let's recap;
Patience can keep you from taking a nap.
Anyone who disagrees with all this
Can go get a life,
For many things they will miss.

JANAI DORSEY

When my grandfather was a little boy, he had many jobs.
Some of them included: Milking cows, feeding chickens, and
making a fire. He did all of these things without any pay, which
taught him a lot of responsibility.

During the time my papa went to school, he had to look
after three children. Even though sometimes he did not want to.
Some of them had not even started school yet. It taught him
patience.

While he was in elementary school, if you were not kind
and respectful, you would not have any friends. "My momma

always said that if you cooperate, you can get the job done."

When my papa's brother was killed in a car wreck, it was very devastating. He was given courage because of his upbringing in the church. It also taught him perseverance.

In conclusion, in spite of his past, he still has his integrity.

LINDSEY SIMPKINS

Kindness and Responsibility

Once there was a little girl named Demasha. One of her friends came over, and her mom was not home. She was still at work. And her friend asked her to go down to the store with her. Demasha said her mom was still at work, and she didn't think she was supposed to go. But Demasha's friend said they would be back before her mom got home. So Demasha said, "OK, like let's go." But they weren't back before Demasha's mom. They came back 2 _ hours later. Demasha's mom was so scared. She said, "Demasha Tianen Stringer, where have you been? I was just about to call the police!" And Demasha's so-called friend ditched her, and Demasha never left without her mom knowing.

SHAMOND STRINGER

My great-grandma told me this story:

When I was 12, a tornado hit Gainesville. The day started like every other day. I go to school and walk back, but today was different. It was a hot day going to school. When I came home, it got cool. My instincts told me that something was wrong. It was very windy. The clouds were gathering in the west. I got scared. I ran in the house. It started to lightning. Then a heavy rainstorm came with hail. The rain stopped. I got happy, so I started to go outside. Then, the neighbor was screaming, "Twister, Twister!"

I ran back in my room. We had to go to the cellar. I was scared. I got stiff, but I put my every bit of courage up. I ran outside and dived in the cellar. Everyone got in. 15 minutes later, it was over. I came out of the cellar, and everything was destroyed.

This story taught me courage.

NICHOLAS JOHNSON

Responsibility is the character trait that my mom learned at a young age. She helped to take care of her sick mother and two younger brothers. She helped with cooking and cleaning because her mother needed her help. This showed what being responsible was all about.

At the age of fifteen, she was asked by her mother's doctor if she felt like she was able to learn to give her mother an insulin shot. That is when she showed much courage. She agreed to come in to the hospital after school and learn how to monitor her mother's sugar level. She would also learn how to draw up the insulin in syringes and give her mother a shot, if needed.

Having so much responsibility was sometimes not a lot of

fun. Yet, she admitted that the experience made her a strong person. She learned perseverance, patience, cooperation, and loyalty. She learned the importance of family. She is able to be a better mom to her children, because she has been blessed with good health, and good character building experience at a young age. It made her the responsible woman she is today.

CODY PARKER

What year were you born?

"I was born in 1925."

What did you do for fun?

"What I done was wash dishes and feed the chickens, and on the weekend, I went and saw a drive-in movie."

Where did you go to school?

"I went to school four years and then stayed home and help my mama."

What age did you marry?

"I married my husband in 1946, and I had 4 children"

What was your favorite thing to do back when you were a teenager?

"My favorite thing to do is to listen to the radio with my dad and mom and oh, did I say my husband died at age 47 with an aneurysm of the brain?"

YANELY RAVELO

En mi país Mexico

En el ano de 1985 en mi país Mexico paso una tragedia un terremoto casi termina con el centro de la ciudad huvo casas derrunbadas, edificios y hospitals mucha gente se quedo sin viviendas y toda la gente se unio para ayudar y coperar que si todos coperamos podemos salir adelante y lenvantar el pais cuando lo nesecita.

La Amabilidad y Respeto!!!!

Yo creo que la amabilidad y respeto es muy importante para cualquier persona y much mas cuando el trabajo de cualquier persona es atender a la demas gente por que una persona amable y respetuosa tiene mas valor como ser humano.

La Perseverancia!!!!

Hace tiempo una amiga de mi mama que estudiaba la universidad esta amiga tuvo un problema que tenia solucion pero ella pensaba que por ese problema tenia que dejar los estudios pero con paciencia y perceverancia pudo salir adelante y terminar su carrea.

La Responsabilidad

Mi trabajo es de mucha responsabilidad muchas veces mi maquina no trabaja y yo se que debo tener paciencia por que la integridad y valor de mi trabajo son lo mas importante.

CASTON DAVIS

Nana Never Gave Up
(Interviewed Barbara Caston)

There once was a woman who quit school too soon,
To marry the man who made her heart swoon.

School had been hard for all the Cook kids,
They were so very poor, no matter what anyone did.

She got no diploma, no college was in the plan,
She wanted to be a good wife to this man.

She spent twenty years doing work that was tough,
Working hard jobs that were grueling and rough.

She wanted so badly to have her own beauty shop,
But she had to keep working-she could not stop.

When the day finally came when her kids were all grown,
She said, "Now it's time for a dream of my own."

She went back to school and studied hard for years,
The hours were long and there were lots of tears.

Her classmates were younger, she was so far behind
But she kept persevering; improving her mind.

Even on the days when her body said "no"
She kept on pushing, she had miles to go.

For her parents had taught her, when she was a child
That life might be tough, but keep going and smile.

She knew what hunger and cold were about
And she knew she would never let failure win out.

She's battled cancer and surgery to her brain,
She's cared for the dying, she's cared for the lame.

She never says "no" to someone in need,
She always keeps going, keeps planting good seeds

And those she has touched learned how to persevere
Not just for an hour, or a day, but for years.

KANIESHA STOVALL

My grandmother showed character basically all her life.
Mary Kesler started showing responsibility at a very young age.
She began when her father died and all that was left was her
mother and all of her brothers. She began being responsible by
helping out with her brothers.

Once she got a little older she began working in a school
cafeteria. That helped her to have cooperation because she had to
cooperate with the other workers so that they wouldn't mess up

any food. Not only did she show cooperation, she showed diversity. My grandmother showed diversity while working in a daycare with all the different types of personalities and ethnicities.

Patience was the key that helped her open all the doors. Mary had to have patience while raising 7 children on her own and putting them through college. There are still other things that my grandmother showed. She is an excellent person.

ALLISON TATE

My name is Lynn Tate, and I was born on April 28, 1965 at Northeast GA Medical Center to Ms. Evelyn Waller and Mr. Gordon Dubouse. Growing up I lived with my grandparents and family. When I got in trouble, my punishments were staying in my room and not being able to watch TV. Usually it lasted 1-2 weeks at a time. While in 10th grade, I had a job at a school program going in 2-5 PM.

My mother worked two jobs. I didn't understand then, but she would always say, "You will do whatever you have to do to take care of what's yours."

She never depended on others to make it through, and she was very responsible for her actions.

My grandfather was diagnosed with Alzheimer's disease, which is caused by degeneration of brain cells. When he came home from the hospital, we knew that it was going to be hectic. He regressed back to his childhood. We knew that we would have to be patient with him. From that, I learned to respect others and their feelings.

Loyalty lies in my family setting. Death always has played a part in my life. It is often sad that families tend to come together at these times.

I had my first child when I was 21 and my second child at 22 and my third child at 26. My brother went in to brain surgery because he had too much fluid on his brain. It was very painful to see this happen. He was very difficult while under medication. Through his cooperation with the doctors and hospital staff, he successfully came out and is doing really well.

I had the opportunity to go to nursing school after my second child. With the help of my parents, I graduated and received my L.P.N. license. My success has been given to me by God. I truly trust that he leads and guides me daily, and I have a lot of success.

JADA CHATMAN

My mom's name is Marie Harrison, who is a wonderful, strong lady. She deceased about 6 years ago of being an ill lady. She did her best to take care of me, my three sisters, and my younger brother. My three sisters' names are Stella Mae, the oldest, Linda, the next oldest, myself, the second youngest, and Elaine, the youngest. We all went through tough times. We had to take turns wearing each other's clothes and shoes when we went to school over at Clarkes Elementary. We attended Clarkes Elementary, located right here in Gainesville, but it is now torn down. We lived where what people call today "the projects". We lived in the projects because that was all my momma could afford.

Everyday, I thank my momma for continuing to raise us no matter how hard it was. Today, all my sisters managed to survive the struggles. My brother became grown and moved to Atlanta, where he was stabbed by his girlfriend. My sisters and I have always said, "The family that prays together, stays together." One of the words I learned through my younger years was respect. I learned respect from my mother by me showing it to her and her showing it to me.

YACCIRI BURCIAGA

I interviewed my grandfather. My grandfather didn't tell me much, but he told me about responsibility. He told me that when he was a little boy, he had to help his father do all the work in the ranch. My grandfather had to wake up early and feed the cows, pigs, horses, and all the animals they had. He also told me that most of the time, he didn't do things that kids his own age were doing. My grandfather said that taught him responsibility.

BLAINE MARTIN

Summers Spent With My Grandparents

This is a story of when my grandma stayed with her grandparents though the summer. She and granddad had a pact every summer. She fed the dogs and would get paid. She would do it every day because Granddad explained to her that the dogs needed fresh water when it was hot. She would do her job, and he would pay her. That shows how responsible she was at a young age.

She stayed with them several summers and when other family members asked her to stay over, she would stay with her grandparents because of her loyalty to them. It took courage to say no to others.

At the time, she had younger cousins, Harold and Dennis, who have always looked up to their big cousin (my grandma). She was patient and kind to them even though they were just babies. Even as an adult her cousins still look up to her and she it still patient and kind to them. She was always a sweet little girl. She has always been willing to do things with the younger kids as well as with her aunts and uncles. She enjoyed doing things like playing with younger kids and did what they liked and enjoyed doing it.

She loved spending time in the kitchen, cooking with her granddad and granny. They taught her how to cook. She always tried to finish what she began and that is a great trait. She had an older brother. He was 10 years older than her. She respected him very much. He helped anytime she needed it.

Her grandparents were wonderful people. She loved them very much and enjoyed every summer she spent with them. They taught her many things and helped make her the wonderful grandmother she is today.

DOUGLAS MCDUFF

Responsibility

This is a story about making responsible choices. In 1974 my father was a Navy pilot based on the aircraft carrier USS John F. Kennedy, flying F-4 Phantoms. Flying off an aircraft carrier is a fairly dangerous occupation, and a pilot is faced with many decisions every time he flies that affect his safety, the safety of the aircraft, and the safety of others.

One night my father was scheduled for a night mission, which has its own particular set of dangers, because taking off and landing from an aircraft carrier at night is a very risky operation. He checked the maintenance log and noted that the center fuel tank on his plane was leaking but had been repaired. The catapult launch was normal, accelerating the F-4 from a speed of zero to a speed of approximately 160 mph in less than two seconds. As he became airborne, all of a sudden there was a tremendous explosion and fire enveloped the entire aircraft. Over the radio, the voice of the tower chief yelled, "F-4 off the bow catapult, you're on fire, you're on fire!"

The normal procedure in a fighter aircraft when it is on fire, particularly at low altitude, is to eject. Instantly, he took his left hand off the throttle and reached for the ejection handle, but he continued flying the aircraft with his right hand never leaving the throttle. He was able to determine that the F-4 was still responding to the controls. So, rather than eject immediately he decided to stay with the aircraft for a few more seconds to see if it would continue to fly. It did not take long for the flames to stop, and the aircraft looked like it was going to fly normally, which it did. After gaining altitude, he checked the plane out thoroughly to see if it was safe to land and then waited for the other planes to launch and returned safely to the carrier. This split second decision saved the $15 million dollar F-4, and no lives were injured. His commanding officer was very pleased with his performance.

Sometimes you are forced to make choices in a very short period of time, and you have to evaluate all the information that is available to you. Some of that information may be telling you to make one choice, but you in your mind have to figure out what the best choice is and the choice that will be the most responsible to yourself and the people around you.

Just like a pilot must make responsible decisions when flying an aircraft, so must everyone in their day-to-day lives. People make decisions that affect their lives and the lives of others, so be responsible!

ARACELI HIDALGO

This story is about this guy named Justin Smith. When Justin was a little boy, he played with his mom's wallet. His mom always told him to leave her wallet alone, but again he was a little kid so he did not pay any attention. So one day, he was playing with the wallet, he decided to take it outside. When he threw the wallet into the sky, and it came back down he couldn't catch it. So the wallet fell on the ground and then the lawnmower passed through the wallet. All of the stuff in the wallet shredded. Justin got in trouble. Justin learned responsibility.

Justin worked in The Hollywood Theater. There was a

guy that was taking his time to do something. So Justin was getting tired of waiting on him, so Justin hit him. The guy fell over this kid with popcorn. The popcorn fell on the kid's mom, but that wasn't it. The popcorn had a lot of butter. So the popcorn left butter stains on the shirt. The lady got really mad. Justin learned patience.

This story is about this man named Joe Bady. When Joe was a little boy, his parents owned a house that was called "section house". It was his house and on the side there were four smaller houses. The four smaller houses were the workers' houses. On the end of one house, there was a pomegranate bush.

One day Joe was walking through and found a pomegranate on the floor, so he decided to pick it up. Joe took the pomegranate to his mom. His mom asked him if he had asked the lady if he could have it. He answered, "no", so his mom told him to take it back and ask if he could have it, and he gave the lady a nickel. Joe learned integrity.

KRISTINA BRAUN

My mom's name is Kim. When she was thirteen, she learned responsibility and courage one night when she was babysitting her two brothers that are younger than her. That night when she put them both to bed, she started watching this murder movie. When she heard a knock on the door, nobody was there. She went back to the TV. There was another knock on the door. She went to the door and still, nobody was there. Little did she know that the person knocking on the door was one of her brothers. He snuck out of the bedroom window. Then he went to go get his b.b. gun. After he got it, he started to scream. While he was screaming, he shot the gun off, which scared my mom to death, but just like any other babysitter would do, she went to go and check on her brothers. Meanwhile, her brothers were climbing back into bed. She was opening the door, and he was already in bed by the time she got there.

REBECCA LAWRENCE

Perseverance
Perseverance is my character word.
I'll tell you a story you've never heard.
My grandmother, Memaw, grew up working hard.
She did chores everyday around the yard.

Memaw was sweet and never would fuss,
Even when she had to walk a long way to the bus.
Memaw had to cook and milk the cows before school.
Perseverance was her family's most important rule.

"Never give up" is what her parents always said,
and her teacher taught her to always use her head.
Memaw was told to always try.
As she got older she understood why.

Sometimes the weather was real bad.
That would make her family very sad.

Memaw picked cotton and worked on the farm.
She had to get up early, so she set her alarm.

My grandmother always wore hand-me-down clothes.
I understand because I have some of those.
Memaw's mother had to gather eggs to sell,
To buy coffee and sugar and other things as well.

Memaw had the most responsibility later in life
When she became a mother and a wife.
She had four girls and one little boy
To teach them responsibility was hard, but a joy.

VENUSTIANO PEREZ

Once there was a boy named Juan. He used to bully people. One day, another bully moved in to his block. He was a big bully. They met in the park. Jack was the bully's name. He wanted to start a fight with Juan. Juan pushed him, and then Jack said, "Why are we bullies fighting against each other when we could get money from the stupid little kids?"

They went walking though the block and saw a boy with glasses. Juan said, "Let's get that geek." They chased the kid all around the block, and soon a dog was chasing Juan and Jack. Juan tripped Jack so the dog could get him. But Jack got Juan from the foot, and Juan fell.

The dog was chasing them, so he could play with them. Then Juan and Jack started laughing. They thought the dog was going to bully them. Juan and Jack shook hands and said, "no more bullying with little kids." The next day, Juan and Jack were playing with all the little kids. I think Juan and Jack learned a lesson from the nice dog.

KAITLIN DELL'AQUILA

Samantha was a girl around the age of 15 when she had to take care of her little sisters, Jenny and Heidi. Her mother and father had to go to a retirement party in another town a few hours away. They told Samantha to be very careful and be responsible. After everyone said their good-byes, they left. Samantha was a few years older than her sisters, but not by much. It was kind of hard since they weren't that young. Samantha got along better with her sister Jenny than she did with Hiedi, so her and Jenny watched t.v. together while Heidi played a little with her dolls. Soon it was time for lunch and they all ate, but Heidi was pickier about what she ate and she argued with Samantha. Samantha told her she could eat her food or eat nothing at all. Heidi ate and then went to her room. Samantha was frustrated by her sister but didn't do anything. Samantha and Jenny spent their time hanging out with each other and waiting for their parents to come home. Soon, they went into the hot tub and stayed to relax. Heidi came out feeling better and asked to come in. Samantha was done being frustrated and let Heidi in with them. After that, they all got along fine and waited for their parents to come home. After a few hours, Samantha's parents finally came home. They said she had been very responsible and they paid her ten dollars. Samantha had learned responsibility from her baby-sitting job.

LONA PANDA

When I come home from school, I have to cook dinner
Responsibility
Before I sat down and did my homework, the house had to be clean and food ready
Responsibility
When the drought came across the land, we had to get our food from other villages
Responsibility

NORMA OLGUIN

When I was around the age of 14 or 15, I became pregnant. Your father made me marry him cause he said that he loved me so much, but when we were married, he didn't show me no love. Some years later, he would always come home very drunk and woop me and push me out of the house with all your brothers and sisters. While we were outside, we would go where I used to wash your dad's clothes and I had my kids there until the next morning when he woke up. I remember when your older sister had to go to school with no shoes and everybody would just laugh at her because of that. It has been 14 years ago when they all made fun of her and all she could do was run and hide where no one would find her and cry. Your father showed me no respect during those 25 years that we lived together and he showed me no respect at all and he showed your brother and sisters no responsibility because he didn't even bought him a pair of shoes, clothes, or a toy.

MARIA PALACIOS

A Childhood Responsibility

Many children do not realize how good they have it. When I was a child, I had to drop out of school to help out my ten other siblings. You might be thinking that this was in the early 1900's, but my story is actually from thirty years ago. You see, in my country(Mexico), our economy is not that great and the law does not require us to go to school.

I was the second woman born into my family, and since my older sister was already married, all the responsibilities were on me. I would wake up at four o'clock in the morning to clean up and cook for my family. After I ate I would go take the dirty clothes and wash it in the river. By the time I was finished, it was time to go home and make dinner. Often I had time to myself, so I could play.

All my family worked hard. My brothers would go to work in the city (which was far away, especially by foot), or work on the farm. My little sisters would go to school and then join my mom in the market. My father worked in a gold mine or stayed home and fixed our land. After their hard work, they would come home tired, sweaty, and hungry.

This went on in my life for all my childhood, from when I was ten to when I was eighteen. I rarely had time to play with dolls, not that we could afford them. My only entertainment was watching soap operas and playing with dolls I made out of mops. Not that I ever complained to my parents. I was happy with what we had, because it was better than nothing.

EDGAR MALAGON

The old days, my grandmother said that it was harsh time. She said that when she used to be young that there will always be fights of battle. She told me that the worst battle was Civil Rights. She told me the wars are not good because a bunch of people died, innocent people, good people. Nobody likes war. My grandmother knows all of these things because she is full of life. She was patient.

BRANDON MANGUM

Responsibility
One day a girl named April stayed after school with a friend
April thought she had some family rules she could bend,
When the babysitter decided April could not be found,
She called her parents and told them to search the town.
Her family looked really hard for April.
They all thought what a peril.
They finally found her on school grounds

She was just playing on the playground.
Everyone was happy
Even her good ol' pappy.
That night April had a lesson on responsibility.
In the future she must make a call
Before she can stay after school at all

ABBY MUSSELWHITE

I was a senior in college at the University of Georgia. I was taking physics, a class with a Chinese and Indian professor; in other words, I couldn't understand a lick of what they were saying! I had to have the class to get into the Medical College of Georgia, so I went and took another physics class at Gainesville College. I had gotten B+ and up all my life and all the sudden I had an F! The professors that I had at Gainesville College were actually understandable! Did I mention that I had also proposed to my future wife? Oh, yeah, a very stressful week! By July, I had taken the course and helped (for a small part) plan a wedding! It was now Friday, the last day of the course (in other words, we get our grades), and tomorrow I was getting married!!! Even more stressful!! It was the end of the day...I GOT A B+!!!! I was so proud of myself! I felt so relieved! I finally achieved my goal!!! I persevered!!!

SHA SHIELDS

Responsibility, as told by Betty Lewis

Did I have a job, chore, or responsibility that helped me understand responsibility? Lord, yes! As a young girl I learned responsibility for the rest of my life. I went to work right after school. I was only thirteen. I had experienced being a wife and mother as a teenager.

It was a hard job, but somebody had to do it. When I got married, I had only one child. After her, three more came along. We lasted up until they were grown or grown enough. "We" is my husband and I. They are my children. My husband and I are now separated, but please believe I still have much love for him. Sometimes I had to take care of him. That's how I learned responsibility.

CHARLESTON TROUTMAN

Diversity

From north to south
The move was far,
Fourteen hours
In the car,

The change of color
Was very new,
Exciting to me
A different hue,

Different from me
Yet the same,
I was naïve
To the rules of the game,

I was invited to take a smoke
Behind the school,
I would do anything
To make myself cool,

She and eight girls
Pushed me down,
They threatened and hit
As I lied on the ground

A respected senior
My shining "white" knight,
Rounded the corner
To end my plight,

William Fripp
Gave me his hand,
Black and white joined
A shift in the sand,

It was a new beginning
A mingling of hues,
Black and white together
We had nothing to lose!

PERLA MOJICA

Mi abuela tuvo a su padre y a su madre perdio a su padre. A los 8 anos y empezo a sufrir mucho. Su mama tuvo que trabajar y no le alcanzaba el sueldo y a los 10 anos tuvo que darla con una senora. Crecio con esa senora muy feliz. Se caso a los 17 anos. Tuvo 7 ninos y una hermosa nina. La nina era la mas querida por el abuelo pero murio a los seis meses. Luego mi abuelo se fue con otras senoras luego regreso y le pidio perdon a mi abuela y lo perdono luego a los anos murio su hijo que se llamaba Juan lo mataron en una feria ahora en el 2003 mataron a su hijo Paulino lo asaltaron y lo mataron en el mes 30 de agosto esta es la histori de mi querida y apreciada abuela.

ZENON GUTIERREZ

My Grandpa's History

He told me that when he used to go to school, he had to go walking. And that it was far, and sometimes it was cold. He didn't have a coat, and they had to go early in the morning so he could get there in time just for first period. It was very dark because they didn't have lights so they could see, and he said that sometimes people used to take horses, bikes, and those who had money could go on taxis. And he said that when they went to lunch, he didn't like the food because it was corn and chicken. And he never went to high school over there. He only stayed in 8th grade.

NIESHA BELL

My mom was born in Hall County on Oct. 5, 1973 to Mr. Michael Hall and Barbara Faulker. They named her Lakisha Deanne Hall. When she was growing up, she lived at 1067 Myrtle St. She attended Enota, Fair Street, GMS, and GHS. At the age of 15, she had her first child, me, Niesha Bell. At the age of 19, she had her 2nd child, Talasha Glasper, and at the age of 26, she had her 3rd child, Michael Hall. Now at 29, she works for a church daycare and she takes really good care of me and my brother and sister! And she said back in the day, the schools and how she lived was not like today.

BRANDON CROWL

The Challenger Disaster
My mother was at work when the NASA Challenger Shuttle caught on fire. She and her employers heard about it, and they turned the news on to see what happened. "We just got word from NASA that the Challenger has just exploded," the news channel said. They were puzzled and very devastated. It taught her kindness, respect, and courage in many different ways.

SAYRA GARCIA

I interviewed my parents. Their names are Cristina Garcia and Jesus Garcia. They were both born in Mexico. I asked them what their responsibilities were. My mom said that she had to get up early and go to the chicken house and get their eggs. Then feed them. Then she'd go feed the cows and the other animals. After that, if she had any dirty clothes, she'd have to go to the river and wash her clothes by hand. If there were people, she'd have to wait 2 to 3 hours. She also had to be patient and wait for the other people to wait. If she left, she'd get in trouble. Now my dad had a big responsibility with my grandpa. He had to wake up very early and go help my grandpa in the ranch. He said that he had to be patient because if he got unpatient, he'd get mad. He also had to be patient because sometimes til 1:00 AM. There are the responsibilities they had and why they had to be patient. So they were very responsible and had a lot of patience.

KEONDRA FLENTALL

Courage
Courage is to me bravery,
Love, helpfulness, courage
Having respect for people
Above you never to get mad
Always being glad, always
Cooperating with the chief
And never in disbelief, so
What am I talking about?
Courage! And nothing less.

TURQUISE ANDERSON

The family member I interviewed was my Nanny's husband, and I asked did he know anything about the community of Gainesville back in the day. He said, at Fair Street Elementary, when he used to go in 1953 I think, he said, they had 5th through 9th grade. Then, after that, that's when you go to high school, which is 10th and 12th. But he said, back then, they didn't have computers or none of this technology that we have today. Then he told me that in Townsquare, they had an ice cream parlor.

What this message is saying is that whatever goes on like they said, even though through segregation when people call my Granny bad names and stuff, she didn't fight or retaliate. She got mad sometimes but still kept her head up even though it was tough. Like my Uncle Jerry and them, she never gave up but kept her head up.

CHARLIE NEWMAN

The Courage of a Hero
My Papa, John Yarbrough is one person I admire, love, and respect. I think of him as my hero because he is one person who has shown a lot of courage in his life. I call him Papa John, even though he is not kin to me. He is now 80 years old and has always thought of me as his grandson. He is also one person who is a great example of courage because he fought in World War II when he was only seventeen years old.

John F. Yarbrough was a soldier in World War II from

January 1941 until January 1945. He served in the Army for the whole time that the war lasted. His rank when he got out of the military was as a First Sergeant, but he also served as a Drill Sergeant. Mr. Yarbrough felt proud to be a part of the military because he felt that Americans needed to support their country. He was very young, only seventeen years old, when he joined the National Guard. He had been a member of the high school band in Tuscumbia, Alabama, and loved music. His band teacher, Dick Roberts, and several of his friends in the band all joined at the same time. This shows great courage because he was so young but was willing to leave his family and fight for his country.

Mr. Yarbrough had many interesting experiences during the war. He was first stationed in the Aleutian Islands near Cold Bay, Alaska. One of his jobs was to be a bandsman and play music for the army. Mr. Yarbrough started out in the 151st combat engineering regiment. Another job in Alaska was to help build an air base and loading docks. The living conditions were very poor. For example, the soldiers had to live in 16 square feet huts with nine men in one hut. He told about one man going crazy because it was so bad to live there. One day the man, whose name was Rollins, grabbed a 45 gun and was waving it trying to kill the enemy. Rollins kept saying, "Where are they? I'm going to kill them!" Papa John showed courage because he had to survive poor living conditions and keep a good attitude.

Sometimes courage includes being scared and dealing with bad things happening. This happened to Mr. Yarbrough when he was in Germany in 1945. He had lost a wire crew (a group of people whose job was to string wire between field artillery and headquarters) and had gone out to search for them.

They were on a dirt road and he heard guns firing behind them and in front of them. They had gotten ahead of the infantry and right in the middle of Germans firing at them. He said at that moment, he realized what war was all about. He said, "that scared my mule!" Also, Mr. Yarbrough told about another time in Germany in 1945 when he almost got killed. Two of his men were going to take a break and go tour a castle nearby. He had planned to go with them, but at the last minute, he decided not to go. The men hit a land mine, and blew their whole truck up! He said he was very fortunate that he decided not to go.

Courage also means dealing with change and facing the enemy in wartime. During war times, Mr. Yarbrough said that things change quickly. For example, he was transferred to many places, such as Louisiana for marching and more training, Texas, Missouri, and California for amphibious training. In Europe, he was stationed in Germany, Japan, France, Belgium, and Holland among other countries. He wound up at the end of the war in Czechoslovakia facing the Russians. What is so interesting is all the places to which Mr. Yarbrough traveled to and how young he was! When he went off to war, he was only four years older than I!

In conclusion, Papa John is a great example of courage because he was willing to fight for his country when he was only a boy. During the four years he was in the Army, he had to survive harsh conditions that most people could not stand. He also had to live in many countries and survive attacks on his life. When he came home, he got the GI Bill and got an education at Auburn University. He is the best example that I know of courage.

KATE VALPEY

Through My Mother's Eyes

He was too

Young,

But it still

Happened.

They said it was

His heart.

He lived for

Five years,

Alive, but not

Really

There.

We came from

All across

The country

To

Stay with our

Mother,

While our

Father

Died

In

A nursing home

At fifty-four.

We came

Together

During

The time
When
Life
Stood
Still.

KANEESHA BAILEY

Responsibility

     My mom told me she learned responsibility when she got her first dog named Roo-Roo. She had to walk her, feed her, give her a bath, take her to the vet. Roo-Roo taught her how to share and to be a mother. A dog is not a toy. You just can't play and trash it. It's more like a baby. And trust me, it is not easy raising a dog or a baby, you really have to care for it. Roo-Roo died one day, and my mother cried because he was like one of the children. And that's how my mother learned responsibility.

ROBERT HUGHES

If you're having a long day
And you're in a bad mood,
Patience is the key.
If you're a teacher
And your students are not cooperating,
Patience is the key.
If you're in a meeting

And you have a headache,
Patience is the key.
Patience is the key.
Patience is the key.

KERRI CHAPMAN

My dad, when he was 13 or 14, he had a lawnmower business. He started out with a push lawnmower and he did two or three lawns a week. He saved up money and bought a better push mower. Then he did more lawns and saved the money. Then he bought a riding lawnmower and did even more lawns. Then he did that for a while and saved up enough money to buy a car. When he went to buy the car, he paid cash for a 1970 new Beetle.

ED HOLLIS IV

Perseverance

When my granddad was young, he wanted a bike, but he knew his mom couldn't get it. He kept asking and asking, and she couldn't. Our first cousin had one. My granddad asked could he ride it, so my first cousin said he could have it.

My granddad had a responsibility. That was to get in firewood and get coal, make up his bed, feed the chickens and pigs. It was hard for him to give instructions. He showed him how to do it on paper and he learned how to do it.

In 1948, they had a big snow storm. One family didn't have wood to burn in their house. So his brother took some slabs down to the person's house so they can have some heat. They were a real close community and they liked most of the people in the neighborhood.

LUKE HICKMAN

When my father was younger, maybe in his teens, he and his friends decided to play a prank on some of the students in his school. They gathered some money, and they went shopping. They drove just outside the border of Georgia and stopped by a roadside shop. They used the money they had saved up to buy some "cherry bombs." They returned to the school, where they strategically placed the "bombs" in the toilets in the restrooms that were in front of the cafeteria. They then flushed the toilets and ran out. When the bombs exploded, the wall of the cafeteria fell to the floor. They all kept running, not even knowing what they had done.

This story may not show that they had responsibility, but they did accept their consequences. The worked together to complete this mischievous deed. They helped clean up the mess in the cafeteria, and then were suspended for forty days each. And I'm sure most people remember the wall coming down.

LILA KATE COOLEY

When my dad was a kid, he learned a lot about responsibility, patience, loyalty, and perseverance. Let me tell you about it.

When my father Jody was nine years old, he was accused of stealing. The store manger said that he had taken a piece of bubble gum, but he didn't. Jody's father took him back to the store and convinced the manager that he was innocent. His dad was loyal.

When Jody was ten, he was in his church's youth group. In his youth group, there was a crippled girl named Suzanne Nichols. He thought that she showed a lot of perseverance, because she had braces on her legs but never let them get her down. People would make fun of her, but she didn't let them get under her skin.

Jody was a Boy Scout for four years. He and his friends were unruly and loud. The Scout Master could have given up, but he didn't. He could have quit, but he didn't. He waited for the boys to mature, and eventually, they did. He showed a lot of patience.

When Jody was thirteen, he had to earn his own pocket money. His father bought him a lawn mower, and Jody pushed it all over town to make money. He had to be on time or a customer wouldn't hire him again. This taught him responsibility.

When Jody was sixteen, he got a job at a local drug store called Burke Drug Company. His job was to deliver the right medicine to the right people. Because he had to drive, he was also in charge of the company car. He had to keep it neat and clean.

It was his responsibility.

In conclusion, my dad learned a lot when he was a kid. All of the things he learned have helped him do well and succeed in life.

PATRICK STOKEY

I decided to do my essay on my sister who uses several of these traits in her job. My sister works as a camp coordinator for a YMCA resident camp. On a day-to-day basis, she uses traits such as cooperation, kindness, respect, responsibility, and patience.

One day, she had a very upset parent call because they felt like their child was not well respected at camp and didn't receive the "royal treatment". This woman was very ugly and spoke harshly and verbally attacked her. Due to my sister's character traits, she had patience with the woman to hear her out and the respect for her not to be ugly back to her. In turn, she took this patience and respect for the woman as an adult to be kind and worked with her to smooth the situation over and make a compromise.

KEVIN GALAVIZ

1. Well, when I (my uncle) was about 15, I was at a party and my friend was shot because some drunk kids killed him while they were playing with guns. Later that night, he died in my

arms.

2. A woman was killed by an oncoming car, and the woman didn't even stay. She left the scene. It taught me (Kevin) that you should always watch out and take care of yourself, and that if you know yourself, and that if you know that person, be sure to be by their family's sides when they grieve.

My Uncle telling:

The divorce of my brother and his wife six years ago, everyone was depressed, and we waited patiently to hear the news, but I don't get it. They were so loyal to each other.

If you don't know the way
Help somebody
It doesn't matter who
Can be anybody
If they're in tough times
They'll turn to you
The person who had helped them
When they were blue

STEPHANIE OLSON

The Garden

One spring day, my father would give me a dime and a long list of vegetables we were going to plant. I then peddled on my bike to the convenience store. Using the list, I bought an array of fruits and vegetables.

Eager to get home and plant, I sped off on my bicycle.

When I got home, I helped father plant the fruits and vegetables. We had to trowel a small ditch, put fertilizer in each of them, drop the seeds in one by one, cover them with dirt, then water. If that's not a tiring job, I don't know what is.

Well, during the summer, my responsibilities for the garden did not cease. Everyday, I went out and watered it. Every other day, I weeded it. I felt like I was the only one caring for the garden. Why wouldn't my father or sister help me with it? Okay, maybe my sister had obligations to fill, such as school and church. But then why not father? I decided to keep these questions in the back of my head, but nonetheless, they did pop up time and time again.

Fall is the time of harvest, in which many families can enjoy fresh produce. For me, the fall was when I went out to the garden and harvested the many different yummy treats. I knew they were yummy; after all, I cared for them that much, and I wanted to know what everyone else thought of them, too. Compliments like "yummy!" and "Delicious!" and "Scrumpdiliumpshious!" floated my way, and I was proud. I realized that if I hadn't cared for them, none of these praises would have been spoken; none of the vegetables would have been alive.

After the meal, father told me to take of the harvest what the family did not need, and to sell the produce for a dime each. I obeyed, and the next day, did so. After selling many vegetables, I spotted my father. "Here are the earnings that I have made," I said. He told me to keep the earnings. He said they were mine! That was my spending money, and I had raked in five dollars at least. So that was why the garden was my responsibility to care for. Are we going to plant one next year? If so, I can't wait!

ELIZABETH MOORE

Pisgah National Forest
It was almost winter, late in the fall,
I was but thirteen and not very tall,
There were twenty of us in the scout troup
And we planned a day hike with our group.
We didn't know that we would be
Learning a lesson in cooperation that has stayed with me.
Before we knew it, we were lost.
It was getting dark and soon it would frost.
Soon it was pitch black, and we couldn't see
We only had one flashlight, and it belonged to me.
We had to find a place to sleep
Until the dawn would us greet.
With only one light, we had to climb
Up the mountain in a straight line.
The only way to stay together
Was to hold hands like a rope or a tether.
So we started up the mountain, blind as could be
And only the one with the flashlight could really see.
After an hour or so the light began to fade
So we had to stop and camp was made
Since we had no light to gather wood,
We did the only thing we could.
A fire was started and from its small light,
We could see to gather enough wood for the night.
One by one, we each fell asleep
But the Scoutmaster stayed awake to watch his sheep

Sometime in the night, I rolled into the fire
My jacket was melted, but nothing more dire.
Finally the dawn came, cold and bright
And we looked down into the valley and saw a wonderful
    sight.
Our cabin was there just a few miles away
But we never would have found it without the light of day.
Without helping each other and doing what was right,
I'm sure some would have perished during the night.
But because we worked together without seeking glory
I am alive today to share this story.

Story by Reid Moore
Poem by Elizabeth Moore

SCOTT LEFEVRE

Perseverance

When my dad was in elementary school, he wanted to
play the accordion more than anything. With much persuasion,
he talked his parents into buying him one and took lessons for a
few years. Even though he wanted to take lessons, he was tempt-
ed to quit because all of his friends were out playing ball and having fun late at night while he was barricaded in the house, practicing his accordion.

When he was fourteen, he worked at a café and earned
money and food for his family when they came to watch him play.
He played only a few nights a week and sometimes he would

adjust his schedule so he could fly some places with his dad. All-in-all, he had to persevere to take the lessons and to work and earn money instead of going out and playing baseball or football with all of his friends.

My dad was the only person to buy his own car with his own money. So he had to take his money from the accordion and buy his first car. Even though it wasn't much, it got him to and from; and that's what matters. Through all of these years, he wouldn't of made it without the help of perseverance.

RANDY SOLOMAN

Kindness is the quality of being gentle, caring, and good towards someone. My nanny (grandmother) had an experience that taught her to be kind. This experience took place when she was young.

In 1963, my grandmother was in the fifth grade. One of her classmates, whose name was Tommy Collins, saw his father, four brothers, and sister drown. Tommy Collins and his family went out to Laurel Park where it runs into the lake. Tommy went out into the lake and got caught in the undertow. His father went out and tried to save him. Tommy's four brothers and sister followed. All of them got caught in the undertow and drowned, except for Tommy. Tommy felt guilty because his daddy went out to save him, and he drowned himself.

This incident taught my grandmother to be kind to Tommy. Not only did it teach her to be kind to him, it also taught her to be kind to anyone. This incident also taught me to be kind to everyone too, no matter what the circumstances were.

EVAN KING

Deck Building
The deck was high
Almost to the sky
It was me and my dad
That made me mad
I learned cooperation
I learned responsibility
Until I didn't help one day
My dad was hit by a board
So I felt it was my job to finish the deck
It took me two weeks
I proved to my dad
I was not too bad

ALEE BOYCHUK

Mt. Rainer
One summer, my dad climbed Mr. Rainer. The story of
his adventure represents cooperation, respect, loyalty, courage,
and perseverance. I think my dad mostly learned about teamwork and trust in his fellow climbing partners.

Mr. Rainer is located near Tacoma, Washington. The
mountain reaches a peak of 15,000 feet above sea level. My dad's

trip involved a two-day climb. Prior to the actual climb, he attended a three-day class to learn life-saving procedures, such as how to stop yourself when you slide, how to climb up solid ice cliffs with ropes, and how to avoid frostbite.

On the first day of the climb, my dad had to pack his backpack and head off to the next station, which is at an altitude of 9,000 feet. His backpack was required to contain a cold weather suit, food and drinks for four days, head lamp for night climbing, pick axes for climbing ice, crampons, goggles, sleeping bag, and four liters of water.

His group of about 15 climbers started their first day at 9:00 AM. At first, the ground was covered with slush and snow, with some grass and rocks. At about 7,000 feet, the steepness of the mountain began to increase. At about 4 PM, he reached the mid-station, where he set up camp and prepared for the next day's grueling hike to the summit. At the mid-station, there are no bathrooms or running water. My dad ate cold pizza, freeze-dried meals that he mixed with water, and protein bars. He then slept in his sleeping bag on the hard ground from 6 PM until 11 PM. At midnight, the group began the dangerous and exciting part of their journey. They climbed straight up to the top of a wall of ice.

Prior to leaving in the dark at midnight, my dad put on a rubberized suit, hard helmet, boots with crampons, goggles, and his head light. The climbers are then tied together with a rope in case one of them should slip and fall. This demonstrates cooperation and loyalty. The climbers work as a team, helping and watching out for one another.

My dad said that at several places, he had to walk on a ladder across crevices or cracks where the ice would split, leaving

200-foot drops below. I think this would be a good example of my dad demonstrating the character trait of courage.

During the first hours of the summit hike, the outside average temperature was about 20 degrees below 0. It would warm up gradually after daybreak. The reason the group sets out at midnight is so they reach the summit by 1 PM before any avalanches start from higher afternoon temperatures.

At the top of the mountain, my dad could see the Pacific Ocean, Seattle, Mt. Hood, Mt. Batchelor, and Mt. Saint Helens. At the very top of the mountain, the wind blows at about 60 miles per hour, so they had to watch out for windburn and frostbite. About every hour, they would have to drink a liter of water, so they wouldn't get dehydrated. The trip was about 15 miles long.

I think my dad learned responsibility, integrity, and perseverance because he had to keep going even if he felt like quitting. He treated the mountain with respect, and he looked out for himself and others by constantly watching for falling rocks, frostbite, altitude sickness, and changing weather conditions. He also showed kindness to others as well as patience when waiting for fellow climbers to catch up with the group.

This was definitely a character-building adventure for my dad.

STEPHANIE SAVITZ

Surviving the Hardships

My grandmother has gone through a lot. She has lived through World War II and even the loss of her husband just a year ago. Her past has helped her in the future. This is how her story goes:

I was a little girl, only about 10. We were living during World War II, when they could strike at any point. I had the responsibility of practicing the drill if they attacked. My house was the only house on the block that had a basement, so I had to get all the kids in my basement. That was my big responsibility when I was little.

When I was older, I got a job at a pharmacy. It taught me cooperation, kindness, respect, responsibility, and patience. I had to be respectful to the customers, even if they were not very nice to me.

I did Girl Scouts until I was about 13. Throughout the years, Girl Scouts helped me understand these ten words: Cooperation, kindness, respect, courage, loyalty, responsibility, diversity, patience, integrity, and perseverance, But I probably learned cooperation most of all because we always had to work together.

My grandmother said a quote that I will always remember: "I don't think about not being nice." My grandmother has survived World War II and the loss of her life because she understood those ten important words.

ALEX TURNER

We were assigned to interview a parent or grandparent and ask them about one time in their life they demonstrated cooperation, kindness, responsibility, courage, perseverance, respect, patience, diversity, integrity, and /or loyalty. I interviewed my poppop or grandfather. I first asked him if he could tell me one time in his life he demonstrated one or more of those terms.

He answered, "After having considered my life to be nearly perfect, I had a beautiful wife, three wonderful kids, a nice house, a meaningful career and then being asked to serve as a deacon at church, I was then diagnosed with a terminal liver disease, the only cure was a liver transplant. It took a lot of courage to continue all of life's activities: Work, marriage, fatherhood, and church service. As the effects of the disease progressed, fatigue and itching really wore on my patience and perseverance. After eight years of illness, I finally received a life saving liver transplant. The strength, courage, and patience that I managed to find, as well as the tremendous support I received from family and friends enable me to be alive today."

I remember the weeks he spent in the hospital. I was very small and did not understand, but I knew my poppop was very sick. He was to receive his transplant in Omaha, Nebraska. When he finally received the message that his miracle had arrived, he and my meme flew up to Omaha. My daddy and I came up shortly after. I remember sitting in the waiting room watching the "Sound of Music", awaiting his surgery to finish.

After that, I asked him if he ever contacted his donor family.

He answered, "After having written my donor family anonymously from the hospital, thanking them for the gift they gave me, I wrote a special letter on the day of my daughter's wedding thanking them for giving me the opportunity to walk my daughter down the aisle. About a year later, I got a letter from the hospital with a letter from the family. The letter told me that my donor's first name was Brian, and he was a distant cousin of Elvis Presley and the minister that presided at his funeral also presided at Elvis's funeral. I have mutual friends with the preacher, so I called him and told him my story. He called the family who called me and they wanted to meet. So, I met Paul and Linda, Brian's parents in Tupelo, Elvis's birthplace. They told me much about Brian and that he had a son, John. I have now met John and attended his high school graduation. They currently live in LaGrange in South Georgia."

I met John, Brian's son on several occasions. He once came to one of my soccer games. Brian committed suicide, and I think having my family who loved him, made John feel that his dad though he lost his life, gave a second chance at life to someone else. An article was published in the Northeast Georgia Medical Center's magazine about my poppop and his amazing story. Most of Brian's story is in there.

Once I asked him about the donor family. I asked him how he felt about receiving a life-saving liver.

"I feel good. How can one express how they feel about being given a second chance at life. I like to do volunteer work to tell people about the necessity of organ donation. There are over eighty thousand people waiting for transplants in the U.S. I would like to encourage everyone to sign up to be an organ donor. 'Don't take your organs to heaven because heaven knows we need them down here'."

The phrase, "Don't take your organs to heaven because heaven knows we need them down here" is on bumper stickers, key chains, pens, pencils, erasers, posters, billboards, I think I even saw a snow globe bearing those words. I saw most of these things at the Transplant Games in Orlando, Florida, back in June 2001. My poppop was a participant and a member of Team Georgia. I was lucky enough to be there. It was truly a miracle to see so many people who receive life from others' deaths.

I don't know what I would do without my popup. He is truly an amazing person. I look up to him so much, and I know it took courage, patience, and perseverance to get through what all he has. I also think it took faith, faith that the lord would look after him and that his time was not up, not quite yet.

JOSE VILLALTA

Cooperation
My Life As a Volunteer

On a Saturday morning, in front of John Marshall High School, Elizabeth was sitting patiently. It was sunny and hot that Californian day, although it was early in the morning. Finally, the rest of the volunteers who would also help arrived. Together, they were going to the S.A.J.E., which was an organization to help poor kids. When they arrived, Elizabeth and her friends were ready to work. As they entered, the saw many kids that had an excited look on their face. Elizabeth and the crew got to work. They did art work with the kids and made colorful drawings. They molded clay and made pottery, too. The volunteers made the children extremely happy. Time flew by and soon the crew had to leave. It was a tiring and fun day. The children were very happy and waved good-bye joyfully. Elizabeth and the crew left happily with a job well done. This experience taught Elizabeth cooperation. She cooperated to help the little children which left the children very happy.

LYANNE ALTAMIRANO

As time passes by, I've realized that each of these words play a role, not only in my life, but on other people's life also. If us humans could know the meanings of these words, and practice them, this world would be a better place to live in. There wouldn't be no crimes, no killing, and victims, and of course, no wars.

Life is full of responsibilities, ever since I was a child. I helped my mom in what I could. Even though I was not a big help, I did my best to help my mom. Another responsibility that I had was that I went to school and studied hard to get good grades.

I know this family that the parents did not teach their sons/daughters about the consequences that they never achieved a goal. In other words, their lives were failures.

About a year ago, my dad got very sick. In this situation, I learned how to be patient, because at that moment, I did not have the resources and the time to go to Nicaragua.

About four years ago, a hurricane called "Hurricane Mish" destroyed a big part of Nicaragua, leaving people without any land or goods. This made people have courage to keep trying harder to get back what was theirs.

After studying the answers of these questions, based on the words above, I've learned that it is very important to know the meanings of these words, but it is more important to do them in our way of life. This way, we can learn how to act correctly, because all of this teaches us how to be strong, and to know how to respect ourselves so we can respect others, and also to be responsible. Also, all of these teach us to give the best of us.

CESIA ROMERO

Responsibility

As my father grew up in a small village named La Union in El Salvador, living with only his one parent, his mother was hard. He was the oldest. He needed to be responsible and had to respect his mom. At the age of 12, he finished school and went to work. This was a big responsibility because the money he earned was for his family. He would also care for the cow and chickens that provided milk and food. Now he has become a respected and responsible man, my father.

ELI FRAZIER

When the Tornado Hit Gainesville
Dad
Such a simple but loving word
I was nervous...I was scared
We ran to the a-model ford

Gainesville
Nothing but piles
Piles of nothing
Piles of brick

Bodies
Bodies of people
Bodies of someone who were loved
Bodies of dogs
Bodies of blood

Screaming
Screaming of sorrow
Screaming of lost love

Relief
Relief of my soul
Relief of everything

My dad was alright

1936
When the tornado hit Gainesville
My great grandpa
But his dad

I think that in this, my grandfather showed courage
because he did not know if his father was alive. Kindness because
he helped all of the other people with their loved one. Patience

because he had to wait all the way from Atlanta to find out if his father was alright, and respect to his parents because he must have realized what if would be like if his father was not alive anymore.

GLADIS CRUZ

Palida

Avia una vez una nina pobre y honrrada pero era muy feliz con su failia pasaron ano y una ocacion por desgracia jayecio su padre desde aquella vez para ella todo se abia acabado pero su madre le dijo no te precupes por que alhun dia nos ba no tocar na nosotros pero que la vida sique alelante siguio su vida sigulo studiando despue se enamoro de mateo tuvieron una relacion y tu vieron paciensia paro que se casaran siguiero su relacion asta que el lepidio que se casaran ella lo asecto y se Juntaron Tuvieron a sus hijo y ella dijo hoy sere una madre responsible y hasi siguio su bida bueno eso es todo. Historia de placida.

KEELA GRIFFIN

A Woman of Courage

When my mom was a child, she was selfish and mean. She thought no one cared or understood her. Also, she made very low grades in school and thought she'd never amount to anything. Her way of thinking changed when she went to the job corps. During job corps, she achieved academic excellence and gained the courage to run for campus queen. She said because of her mentor, Mrs. Brinda Tory encouraged her and taught her about integrity. Then she went on to win the talent contest then to winning the regional contest. Now my mother is a woman of God who uses her trials and tribulations to encourage others. Although she is a single parent, she perseveres through prayer and faith in God.

ANDREW REECE

My essay is about my mom and how she learned the values

Responsibility. My mom has to take care of her cat, Mittens. She had to make sure he was fed and had water and his shots. If my mom didn't do her job, Mittens would be sick, hungry, and a pest problem to the neighbors.

Patience. My mom taught four-year-old Sunday school. It helped her to be patient with children when the kids didn't want to listen or interrupt.

Courage. My mom had a teacher that encouraged her to run for student council. She didn't like to make speeches, and it gave her the courage to run for student council. Respect. When we went to Alaska, there were a lot of elderly people in our group. That taught my mom to be patient and to respect elderly people. There once was a saying that the older, the wiser; the younger, the foolish.

Kindness. My mom showed kindness to the Chestatee Church when they went to the mountains and their bus crashed. Her church went to take care of them until their parents got there.

ASHLEY KITCHEL

My grandfather had a lot of responsibilities when he was younger. He had to work on a farm that he lived on.

My grandfather's father insisted that my grandfather worked on the farm that they lived on. He had to do a lot, and that bugged him a little.

My grandfather had to wake-up every day before school at 4:30AM to do chores. He had to milk three cows, get a lot of eggs from the chickens and take care of the vegetable garden. He had to weed it and stuff. He had to take some of the eggs and vegetables and go to town and sell them. Those jobs taught him responsibility.

My grandfather once tried to rebel against his father because he didn't like having so many chores. He was arguing when his mother just flat out said, "Just do it." That got across to him and taught him responsibility, cooperation, and respect for his parents.

My grandfather could remember some incidents that taught him about a lot of the words, but he didn't want to talk about it.

My grandfather couldn't think of any events or tragedies or disasters in his own community at all.

That is my interview with my grandfather. He went through a lot that taught him about those words.

JANETH PAUDA

I interviewed my mom. She said she was born in Mexico with her mom and day before she got married. After she got married, she lived with my dad. Her family didn't have a lot of money. She had to work at a store that was close to her house. She had to wake up at 6:00 AM to help her mom with food and had to do breakfast. She also had to milk the cows everyday. She said in Mexico everybody had to ride on horses cause there was no cars and the cars there were, they were really expensive.

She didn't go to school when she was my age. She had to work. She only got to the 5th grade. When she was 10 years old. When she was in school, the teacher would hit you if you didn't know your division, addition, subtraction, multiplication, and fractions. They would hit you with a ruler on your hands or your butt.

When my mom was 22 years old, and I was 2 years old and my sister was 3 years old, we moved to Georgia. We have been living here for 12 years. My mom said Georgia and Mexico are really different.

ROSIE CORONA

How My Mom Learned Responsibility

When my mom was younger, my grandma abandoned her with her six brothers and a sister. She left them with a mean woman who didn't care if they ate, bathed, or were sick. Therefore, my mom had to take the responsibility to do those things. This went on for about four months, and in those four months, my grandma called twice and promised to come back. That also taught my mom patience. Living with a woman who beat them up and locked the younger ones in tool sheds when they urinated on themselves, my mom never had a toy in her whole childhood except once when she found a doll in an empty house, but the woman took it away and gave it to her daughter. She also killed my mom's dog. After six long months of torture, my grandma came back. My mom's dad showed up once when my grandma abandoned them. After that, my grandma took them out of the state, and my mom never saw her dad again. She doesn't even know if he's alive.

CASSIE BUFFINGTON

I have heard the stories about how rough it was in the old days. I have heard the stories about how hard it was to survive. I never could understand how good I have it until I heard the story about what my grandma went through.

She was six years old when her mother died. She never knew her father or any family on her father's side. All of her aunts and uncles on her mother's side were either dead or long gone.

She had four brothers and sisters. Her two older sisters were grown and married. Her younger brothers were only 2 and 4 years old. She was the third youngest child.

She and her younger brothers moved in with her older sister. Her and her brothers all slept in the same bed, because her sister only had two rooms in her house.

She worked everyday and only went to school when she could. She only made $.10 an hour working at a man's store. She took care of her brothers, because her sister was rarely there.

After living with her sister for nearly seven years, her sister's husband began to rape her. She told her sister, but she did nothing. She then eventually got pregnant at the age of thirteen.

When she got pregnant, she became eligible to stay in government apartments. She took her younger brothers with her, because she knew they wouldn't be treated right.

I try to imagine going through half of the things she went through, but I can't. My grandma had more responsibilities at the age of thirteen than most people do at age thirty.

PHILLIP BERGLUND

Patience is a strong word. My father learned this word as a child when Hurricane Dora hit his hometown. Now it was difficult staying in the basement for a couple of hours but it was good that he did cause all the drift wood imaginable was on the lawn.

"I don't want to," is the term used most often when chores were asked. But back then (whenever it was), you said yes ma'am or yes sir, or red cheeks was for you. That's also responsibility.

In the ocean, near the shore, are these outlets called funouts. Now if you're tall enough to touch bottom, nothing to worry. But if not, you drift out to sea. Once my dad got stuck in one, and he trusted this guy he didn't even know to push him to shore. That's loyalty.

JOHNATHAN ALLEN

On April 6, 1936, at about 7:00 AM, by great-grandfather, Oscar Gilstrap, was working on his 500 acre farm in North Hall County when he saw an amazingly different colored clouds. About 1 hour and 30 minutes later, his wife, Bell Gilstrap, called him in, and told him that a tornado had touched down on the square of Gainesville. He was shocked.

Mr. Gilstrap turned on his radio, and learned it was true that the tornado had wiped out the square and most of Gainesville and most of the town. He thought to himself and remembered the clouds he saw earlier. He also learned that the Hall County Court House had caught fire and killed some 70 workers. Later that evening, he was laying down to go to bed and prayed to GOD, thanking that him or his family was hurt in this disastrous weather.

The next day, the Sheriff came to the door asking him to help rebuild the Courthouse, and he said he would love to. He worked on and off for 7 to 8 months rebuilding the Courthouse and finally finished it. He was thanked by people all over Hall County and felt amazing for what he did.

Mr. Gilstrap learned from this tornado many different traits, including thankfulness, courage, respect, responsibility, and kindness. He learned that anytime he and his family could be taken away, and he became more thankful for everyone. He was considered a great person from the day he helped rebuild on.

The moral of the story is that you need to be more thankful for what you are given. Character Through the Arts is great for our school and community. This was also an amazing date in our community's history.

ANTHONY WILLIAMS

My mom went to school in the 50's. She graduated in 1963. She worked with my grandma, and they were servants for this rich family down the road from them. Mom had my oldest sister and then my brother and me. After a while, the rich folks my mom and grandma worked for built them a house on Candy Cane Lane. It was a house that was made with six bedrooms and two full bathrooms. My brother wrote that the rich people my mom and grandma work for liked both of them and said they were great people. He wrote that he gave them little work to do, and he was very kind and nice. After a few years, it hit winter time, and my grandma was having chest pain. When she went to sleep, my mom thought she was going to die, and one morning, she did. It hurt my mom so much that she wanted to leave, so my aunts and uncles told her that they would buy her an apartment in Gainesville. The next morning after the funeral, we packed up and left, and after we got settled in Gainesville in our new apartment, my mom told us the last story she told her was she was walking and she saw a man running and after he fell, he got whipped to death by his owner because of trying to run away, and she said no more.

TODERICK T. WILLIAMS

Long ago, my mother had a boyfriend. Her parents told her that she couldn't have a boyfriend. So when she went out with her boyfriend, she snuck out through the window. When she snuck back in, her mother was waiting for her. Her mother was in a rocking chair with a belt. When she got in her room through the window, she got caught. Her mother was whipping her until she got tired, and then she fussed her out. Then she was grounded for a month. She couldn't go anywhere. My mother wasn't like her two sisters. She was the bad one. She always got in trouble. Then one other of her sisters did what she did. Then she learned what she was doing was wrong. So she talked to her younger sister so she stopped as well as my mother. That's how she learned respect.

JIMMY NGUYEN

One hot summer day, a girl was in Vietnam. She was on her swing, swinging side to side. The house was near a river. She always would swing near the river and look at the river.

One day, she was on her swing swinging side to side. She saw these boys swimming in the river.

One boy jumped in the river. He jumped in and was dragged down to the bottom. My mom couldn't do anything. She could only look because she was on the other side. The other boys had courage to save him. They saved him in a dangerous way. They had to pull him from the hair. The boy was saved by

his friends. That was a day that my mom will never forget.
Now she knows that courage can be very useful.

KYLE CLEVELAND

Courage, Loyalty, and Responsibility
My grandfather taught my mom the true meaning of
courage and loyalty. My mom was only 23 years old when this
story happened. My grandfather is the mayor of Waverly,
Illinois, a small town near Springfield. Waverly is built on a nat-
ural gas dome. One morning at 4AM, the gas field blew. The
blast was seen as far as Iowa by a helicopter. Everyone was
asleep when grandpa rushed to awaken the family. The black sky
was lit orange, and there was a roaring sound.
It petrified my mom. Grandpa told my mom and the rest
of the family to get in the car and get out of there. He stayed to
alert the rest of the town and try to stop any further blasts. That
pipeline runs through the whole city. If fire were to hit the main
valve, the whole town would have been incinerated. One to two
hours later, mom and the rest of the family returned home.
Grandpa returned home by the townspeople's help. My mom
never forgot that day. That's what taught her about courage and
loyalty and responsibility.

LAKEISHA WRIGHT

As far as the family difficulty, I've learned to appreciate

all that I have and take nothing for granted because I've seen peo-ple that didn't have anything, and sometimes that was the way it was for my family. It makes me want to help others. Last night, my mom was telling me that she used to be spoiled because she was the only child. She said when she was a teenager, she used to sneak out with her friends and go places, and when she would get back, she would be in trouble. My grandmother always told her that she got to have the responsibility to do stuff. She had to earn her right. Both of my parents learned a lot. One of them went to prison, and the other one survived.

What I'm 'bout to tell you learned me alot not to do things. My dad had it rough all his life. When he did something wrong, his dad hit him with a pot or a pan. That's why my dad is kind of stressed on us sometimes. My dad kind of took it. When he got older, he moved out, and him and his brothers lived togeth-er. My dad started drinking and stealing and selling drugs until he got caught. I was real little, and my mom was putting us away to go to bed. He came knocking on the door drunk, but my mom didn't let him in, so he got some ketchup and put it on his stom-ach pretended like get got shot. He went to jail for it. When he got out, he learned his lesson. When he got out, he took me, my sister, and my mom to Gainesville. Now he is the only one that is not in jail. The rest of them are. Now he is a brick mason. He builds houses. We've been living up here for 8 years.

My name is Chaynell Wright, born 1970 December 26 at Northeast Georgia Medical Center. At age 4, I went to Miller Park Pre-School. When I was 5 years old, I went to Enota and headed to Fair Street. From there, to Gainesville Middle and

High School. I was a very hard working student. When I was in 12th grade, I had Chamarcus, my 1st child. I later finished and graduated and started working at Goody's to support my son, Chamarcus. After a year and a half, I had another child. I wasn't able to work during the time because of physical problems. During the time between 1991-1993, I had 3 kids, but in all, I have four smart, beautiful kids. 1994, I started back working. I was working at 2 hotels. The 1st one was Masters Inn. 2nd was Hampton Inn. I left both of them jobs and started working at Wal-Mart, where I'm still working. Out of my life of hard working, I learned to keep working hard and keep God 1st in my life.

SERGIO RUIZ

Isai Gonzalez, my cousin, said that nobody supported him, that he was going to graduate from high school. But he did and he is a happy young man. His story starts like this. The family didn't support him or believe that he was going to graduate from high school, so my cousin had courage and believed in himself. Isai was keeping up his grades and kept trying and trying. He stayed after school to get help. A year later, everybody was happy with him for graduating from high school. He realized that he didn't want to work outside in the sun; he wanted to work in an office. Now, he is happy because he is not working in the sun, and his parents are thankful for his achievement.

JACK SEALS

A Young Man's War
Taken from a South Georgia cotton farm,
He was sent across land and sea to bare arms.
Now the leader of a U.S. platoon,
He wanted to stop this war very soon.
Placed in unbearable ice cold mountains,
He found it was topped off by bullet fountains.
But all the cannon and mortar fire shot at them,
Rang through his mind like an unforgiving hymn.
And still he thrives with strength,
Leading nightly patrols to their final length.
"This is a young man's war," he says,
and the young men that fell, they were the best.
War is not all glory and heroes,
It's courage and loyalty and sorrows.
And although this farm boy has shown plenty of that,
He still is plenty ready to come back.
On the ship home, he thinks through his head,
The next mysterious step in his life ahead.
But before it starts, there's more work to be done,
A trip to Carolina to share tales of a fallen son.

ILSE ESPINO

When my grandpa died. In 1980, my mom's best friend
helped her understand the loss of my grandpa and because he had

to leave her for some reason.

After my grandpa died, my mom had to go to work at a grocery store since my grandma was too old and she had diabetes. My mom started working since she was 14 years old. While she was working, she had to have respect for all customers.

My mom's responsibility was to work, because she had to buy her own clothes, then she wouldn't have money for her supplies back. They were in a big need of money.

My dad had to be patient when my baby sister was almost born, he only had to wait 30 minutes, but for him, he said it felt like a year.

My dad showed cooperation when he saw a big crash, he went up to see in what way he could help part of the accident.

JAY BROWN

My dad is responsible. He is responsible by keeping his grades up. He also did his chores. He also kept being responsible so he could race his dirtbike with his brothers. And being responsible has helped him be organized and smart. And being responsible in his grown up life and being able to have a family, friends, and a good job.

ALEXA MILLER

Have you ever heard the words cooperation, courage, diversity, integrity, kindness, loyalty, respect, patience, perseverance, or responsibility? These words are all very important in character development. If you are wondering what character development is, it is the development of your personality, the person you are on the inside. I know so many people that have such neat, unique stories about their personal experiences in developing their character, but the person that has taught me the most through her stories is my fourth and fifth grade teacher, Ms. Helen Martin. Ms. Martin taught school for over forty years before retiring, without ever missing a day of school. Ms. Martin has inspired me in so many ways, and she has taught me so many things--not only school, but also how to develop a positive character.

      I have always admired the way Ms. Martin told me she first learned to have courage. When she was seven, an older couple moved to her community. They had four sons who were drafted into the Second World War. One of their sons was killed in Iowajima, one of them died from leukemia, and two never returned from the war. Ms. Martin sort of adopted them; everyday she would go and visit them. While she was there, she helped the couple with the chores that need to be done, and in return, they would help her with homework. Ms. Martin told me that this taught her a lot of responsibility in caring for others. She respected the couple a lot because they really taught her about courage and continuing when they had so many personal difficulties in life. Ms. Martin and the couple were special to each other and they depended on each other. As Ms. Martin grew older, she would still carry them to the doctor and grocery store. Ms. Martin cared for them until they both died in the 1970's. This also taught her to care for elders, and elders have always been a part of her. She says, "If you learn to care for elders young, it becomes part of your personality."

One of the lessons Ms. Martin considers very valuable is still a part of her today. When she was in the first grade, she wanted to write with her left hand. Her teacher thought everyone should write with their right hand. When Ms. Martin held her pencil in her left hand, her teacher would grab the pencil, tap her hand with a ruler, and then change hands that the pencil was in. Ms. Martin's penmanship was not that good until the sixth grade. In the sixth grade, there was a writing contest for a free ice cream. This taught Ms. Martin perseverance, because she would get home from school and practice writing. She practiced every night until she started winning every week. Ms. Martin does everything but write in her left hand. She has great penmanship, but it was difficult to learn. Her teacher showed her the value of doing your best.

When Ms. Martin was growing up, she had to do chores, just like we do. Her job was to help work in the yard. She kept the flowers planted and looking decent, and the shrubbery cut. Ms. Martin's mother always told her that you could tell which kind of people you were by your yard. Ms. Martin had to work in the hot sun and was always tired, but she learned that if she was patient, the job would get done quicker and look better. Ms. Martin also did household chores. Her main one was to polish all the hardwood floors every Saturday. Once again, this taught her a lot of patience, because if she was calm and worked hard, polishing was so much easier.

Ms. Martin told me that she thinks responsibility is the most important characteristics you can have. Responsibility includes being responsible for your actions, traits, but without showing responsibility, it ruins your character. Ms. Martin used to (and still does) give us a lot of advice. The piece of advice I remember most from her, was when she told my class we should look at all kinds of people and appreciate them for who they are and the contributions they make. She told us we should not judge people from where they come from or the color of their skin, but what they can give to society and what they can become!

Ms. Martin has always been very special and close to me. I admire her in so many ways and for all the valuable things she has taught me. I know many of the things she taught me, I will take with me forever! I want to leave you with one last piece of advice that Ms Martin taught us, "What is popular is not always right, and what it right is not always popular." This is important and goes along with character development because, usually, it is difficult to do the right thing and to make the right choice. However, for every action, there is a reaction, and for every choice, there is a consequence. What will be your choice for the future?

MANUEL DEOSIO

I learn responsibility by work in six ways in mowing lawns, exterminating houses, changing oil in cars, paint houses, babysitting, and washing cars, so I could raise money to buy a new stereo. But that wasn't enough to buy it, so I got another job. It was household. I had to feed the fish, wash the dog, and don't let the bird fly. So I did what I was told. A week passed, and I was tired. What am I going to do with all this work? I could just call and see when they are coming. "We're back," the lady said. Here's your money I owe you. Now you can leave." Hey thanks a lot. Now I can buy my stereo. I left and still looked for more jobs.

LAURA DEMBY

When my mother was in seminary in the early 1980's, they had almost no female preachers to look up to. My mother got a group of students together. They asked a respected female preacher to come and preach for them and to hold seminars. They created Women In Ministry Week. The students raised $1,000 to pay for the speaker's traveling expenses and hosted a week of preaching and seminars by and about women.

In the midst of planning this special week, my mother faced criticism from some conservative students who thought that only men should be preachers. There were also some who only wanted a radical feminist to come speak. One night, my mother called her father to tell him how frustrating it was. She was surprised when he told her that he knew just how she felt.

In the early sixties, her father had served on the athletic board at UGA. He lead a movement to begin integrating the athletic programs at UGA. Often he was the only one to voice these opinions. He reminded my mother how frustrating it was when the "liberal" professors would tell him after the meetings that they were on his side. "Why don't you speak up?" he would ask them in frustration.

My mother realized that it often takes a long time and a lot of courage and perseverance to promote a culture that accepts and encourages diversity.

CAYLA REECE

On July sixteenth, 1963, Pam Reece was born in Gainesville, Georgia. She is now forty, and when she looks back on her childhood, she realizes how much she learned. She did not only learn academics, but she learned life traits.

In her eyes, responsibility was the hardest one to learn. She got her very first job at "Big-G". She went the day after her sixteenth birthday. She noticed how much work it takes to save money to buy your own car and pay for the gas, but she couldn't give up and stop working.

Pam was always good in school, and she always tried hard at it. When her senior year came along, she let her grades slip in math. Her math teacher, Ms. Kelly, always told her not to quit and to always stay at the top of the class. Ms. Kelly taught Pam perseverance.

One trait Pam was lacking was patience, but that changed when she volunteered, at age nineteen to work at a crisis hotline place. She would spend all night listening to people talk, because they were lonely or depressed. She learned patience, kindness, and respect from that one job.

Looking back on your childhood, you probably now see you learned some of life's most important things. You learn academics and character traits. People judge you by your traits that stand out. These traits are something very important that will help you in life.

ALLISON SHULER

Responsibility

You know many people who are responsible. Your teachers, your parents, and your grandparents have to be responsible. You see them acting responsible everyday. Did you ever wonder why or how they started acting responsible?

Sometimes, it may be because of a family situation, like it was with my grandmother. She was the second child in her family. When she was seven, her father became very ill. Her mom expected my grandmother to take care of her younger brothers and sisters, and help clean up the house, while her mom was at work.

When you have a father who is ill, you need to help out as much as possible, like my grandmother did. She went to help out the elderly to get some extra money for her family. She helped clean their houses and take care of them. When she was eleven, her mother sent her each month to pay all the bills. My grandmother had to walk to all the buildings to pay the bills. When she got old enough, my grandmother went to work at a dime store during the day and then she went to night school to get an education.

There was one person who really made a difference in my grandmother's life. One lady she worked for helped her out a lot. My grandmother didn't realize it at the time, but the lady needed her help. She would give my grandmother the money she needed for the next week's lunch and talked to her the whole time. She told my grandmother how important a good education was.

My grandmother lived through many tragedies in her life. She was a very little girl during The Depression and she said she didn't remember it very well. The major tragedy that she remembered was World War II. She said that made the greatest impact on her life. She helped around the town by collecting newspaper, scrap metal, and rubber. Everyone in the town helped out. They would bring everything to the school and then service workers would come and collect everything. One time, the newpaper came and took a picture of the metal. Another way my grandmother helped out during World War II was by knitting squares to make blankets. Her class called this project Bundles for Britt's.

My grandmother has learned many things from tragedies. The main one was responsibility. She realized that everyone can teach you a lesson, even if they don't realize it. The main thing she told me was, "I can learn something from everything I do."

DREW BLAKLEY WHITMIRE

Story of Rick Whitmire

1. Patience: My mom and dad wanted me to start piano lessons when I began the second grade. I first got started and the first thing that I did the first four weeks was cut my wrist open. I had been playing with friends and I fell down a bank and landed on an old piece of glass. It was bad enough that I had to get stitches and wear a cast for six weeks. After that was over, I con-

tinued my piano lessons, which I hated, though I loved piano. Through the ten years I took piano lessons, they were boring and long. After doing so, I became one the best students in my piano class. When I was 13 years old, my band played at all of our middle school dances. Later, I joined a band called Shiloh, with one of my friends who is now the lead guitarist for Travis Tritt, Wendall Cox.

2. The Lawn Mower: When I was younger, I had a little business of my own. After I was done riding my go-kart in the summer time, I would switch the motor off of my go-kart, onto my lawn mower. After doing so, I would cut people's yards for money. If I did a good job, I'd get paid more. If I slacked off, which rarely happened, I'd get paid less money.

3. Kindness Counts: I remember one day a while back, I had a friend who wasn't the most popular guy. His family was very poor, and for that reason, he was made fun of. He couldn't afford all the nice clothes like all of the "popular" kids. No one thought anything about making fun of him, until one day, he had his head out of the window waving at some friends, and the bus driver turned a corner pretty sharp. When it did, the bus scraped the side of a telephone pole, along with the boy's head. It crushed his head between the pole and the bus, and all of the people who made fun of him had been very sorry about how they had treated him. Now he was gone, and no words could be said to make up for how they treated him.

SEARA BUFFINGTON

Even though she finished high school with the responsibilities of having a child, she had to be very patient. Patience would be the key word that you need. Handling a child, especially at 15 is really hard and requires a lot of patience.

At a younger age, 8 years old, Tasha learned how to have courage. When she was eight, she was struck by a car, breaking her femur bone in two. She was in the hospital for 3 months. She had to take physical therapy. With a lot of courage, she had to learn how to work. That had to take a lot of courage.

With Tasha becoming a young mother, she knew that she would get a lot of negative attitudes. That's why Tasha shows all of these: Responsibility, patience, courage, positive attitude. She has learned a lot of life lessons. That's why she's my mother.

TANISHA HILL

Cooperation, Kindness, Loyalty, Responsibility, and Courage
Once upon a time, there was a little girl named San. All she would think about was basketball. Basketball was her life all through middle school. She played basketball, but when she turned fourteen, disaster struck. Her parents were having problems, so they decided to get a divorce. San showed a lot of responsibility because her mom was really sad and sick over the divorce. When San got into high school, she played basketball with her two best friends, Cayla and Sydney. They all loved to play basketball.

They were the starring players. They could play really good. During practice, San, Cayla, and Sydney thought that they did not have to play and they thought that they could just joke around and say negative words about the other players. They just thought they were the best. So one day, the coach told San, Cayla, and Sydney to shoot twenty free throws and how many they miss, the whole team has to run as many laps as they miss. So San went up first and made eighteen out of twenty, Cayla made eighteen, and Sydney made only five out of the twenty, so the team in all had to run nineteen laps. San and her friends learned that they have to have cooperation and be nice to the other players.

Later, about six months after that, San got a job at Pizza Hut, and she said, "you have to show kindness to people that you really don't like." She also said that "it is hard to be nice and patient to people that you really don't get along with."

A couple of months went by and San and a girl named Keisha got really close, and they became best friends. San and Kiesha would do everything together, but one day, San got tired of hanging out with Kiesha so much, so she would go to the mall, movies, and joy riding by herself. San's favorite cousin said one day, "don't take your friendship for granted", meaning don't neglect or put things before your friendship and don't assume that it is always going to be there. That made San think and show more loyalty to her friendship with Kiesha.

About a decade later, San got married and had two kids named Ethan and Hannah. Hannah really wanted to go to Brownsville, Florida, just to get out of the house. When they got there the family went to a revival. It gave San so much courage.

It showed her something about God. Before then, San never knew if God was real or not but during the revival, she saw him move in powerful ways.

ANDREW AIKEN

This story is about my mom, Debbie Aiken. She was born and raised in Gainesville, Georgia, with two working parents. This story tells about how she developed character traits, such as, responsibility, respect, and loyalty.

Debbie's parents raised her to be respectful to them and other adults. Being the oldest child, she was given the responsibility of looking over the house and her siblings while her parents worked. It was important to do the very best she could while watching over her siblings, so her mom didn't have to worry. Because they didn't have a washing machine, Debbie had the responsibility of going to the Laundromat. She did all this plus regular daily chores. Because of her responsibility, her mom trusted her to go out and play in the neighborhood.

To earn extra money, Debbie babysat kids across the street and ironed her neighbor's clothes. These two things show responsibility. When she went to the store, she would ask the elderly people if they needed anything. She was responsible enough at the age of fifteen to get a job.

When she got home from school, she had to do homework before doing anything else. She was responsible and studied to make good grades in school. After high school, she did night classes to further her education. Debbie eventually earned a degree in computer programming.

ZACH BENNETT

1. The day that the tornado tore through Gainesville in 1936, my grandmother was eleven and lived in Dawsonville. She remembers her father giving a man a ride to Gainesville the day the tornado hit. The man wanted to see if his family was hurt or safe. My grandmother rode in the car and saw her father's kindness toward the man.

2. My grandmother, who is 79, said she never had a special job or chore when she was a child. She said if there was a job to do she did it without being asked to. If her mom had to go to the spring house (a small building built over a creek where food could be kept cool) she would go along to help.

3. My grandmother was a freshman at Brenau College. She was a member of a choral singing group which was performing for the cadets at Riverside Military Academy. Colonel Sandy Beaver was the head of Riverside. He interrupted the performance with a very serious announcement that my grandmother will never forget. He said he had just been informed that the Japanese had just attacked the United States Navy at Pearl Harbor. She looked around at all the young cadets and thought about the courage of the great military men.

4. My grandmother said that her father ran a general store across the street from their house. Sometimes her father would lock up the store during the day and come home to work in the garden or help with their six children. If a customer needed help

in the store, they would ring a large bell outside the store to let her father know he was needed. My grandmother said he sang at funerals and helped anyone who needed food or money. She learned integrity from him.

5. One morning, my grandmother was getting ready for school. She walked outside and looked up at the sky. She said the sky looked in a way different than she had ever seen it before. It was almost black. When she came home from school that afternoon, her father told her a bad tornado had hit Gainesville. He drove to Gainesville (she went with him) to offer his help. She learned responsibility and cooperation from him.

The year was 1936. She was eleven years old. One day, she woke up and looked up at the sky and it looked very strange. She had to walk to school but the air was so still and quiet she was nervous. The birds were not singing. She had a bad feeling and she didn't know why.

When she got to school, her friends were talking about how dark the sky was. They tried to get to work but continued to look out the windows at the dark, black sky.

After school, she walked home and there she heard her mom and dad talking very seriously. They told her there had been a terrible tornado in a town 35 miles away.

Her father drove a man all the way to the devastated town to see about his family. She rode along with the two men. When they got to the town she couldn't believe her eyes. Trees and buildings were broken and torn apart. People were walking through the destruction and they looked like they were in shock.

Her father drove the man as close to his family home as

possible. They had to stop and get out of the car because the streets were covered with trees and debris. The man pointed to a house. He began to run toward the house. There was a woman standing on the porch. She was crying. The roof had been blown off. The man hugged the woman.

She was afraid to look at the woman. She was so frightened and sad. She was sorry the tornado had come through this town. Homes were blown away and people were killed. She was very proud of her father for helping these people.

MADDIE HOLLISTER

Beep…beep…beep…beep…beep…goes the heart monitor over and over. One hour later beeeeeeeeeeeeeeeeep, a straight line.

There was a very miserable and depressed little girl who has a heartbreaking story. It all began when this little girl, Mary, the youngest of three, came down to breakfast. When she got there, she was surprised to see her mother weeping to a great extent. When this little girl asked what was wrong, her mother simply replied, "I cannot say."

Mary had a horrible feeling that it was something bad. All of the following days, this little girl named Mary felt as if something was hanging over her shoulders. She was in a world of bewilderment. She had no idea.

As this little girl became not so little, she was told that her eldest sister Jane had a terrible problem. She had breast cancer. When Mary realized the reality of her sister's disease, she had a sudden feeling of emptiness. Like nothing else could be worse. This day had come to be the worst day of her entire seventeen years of living.

These past months, Mary had to have a lot of courage. Mary had to live with the fact that her sister Jane, the Jane who saw Mary through thick and thin. She had lost her very best friend. That Jane was going to die. Mary had to be very brave and very helpful.

Jane was checked into a hospital and Mary was asked if she would like to go and see her sister. Mary simply replied, "I do not want to go. I just cannot bear to see her like this." Eventually, after a very hard five years later, her dearest sibling, Jane, got better, or so Mary and her family thought…

Her wellness did not last long: She was back in the hospital three years later, and the cancer was back with a vengeance. Mary went to se her yet again, but what she did not realize was that it would be the last. On November 13, 1992, her beloved sister was declared deceased. Mary was at home when her family got the call. The entire rest of the night was filled with wadded Kleenex and never retiring sobbing.

Now, Mary's life is much different, and she will never forget that day. She has moved on with her life, and she herself has matured a great amount. As she goes on, that day will always live on in her heart. She will always remember.

AMANDA BACHE

A story my mom told me about when she was in middle

school is when she worked at a barn. She had to be very responsible for this because the gorses had to rely on her. She had to clean the stalls, feed, water, turn out, and bring them back in. Horses have sensitive stomachs, so if my mom fed them late, it would make them sick. Horses also drink 7-12 gallons of water a day during the summer, so my mom had to keep them watered.

STEPHANIE WALDRIP

Since everyone expected them not to do so well, that only drove them even harder. Flat out determined the football team worked all summer long, carried blocks in the hot summer heat, running two to three times a week, working out daily, and all this on top of training for football itself (football practices, etc.)

The season rolled around and all the hard work started paying off. No one ever would have expected the Gainesville High School football team of '68 to make it all the way to the state championship game! They did, and they proved everyone wrong.

Final game day came, and the weather was bad. It was rainy and humid. The field was soaked and muddy as can be, but the game was still played. In the end, GHS came out with a 6-0 loss. That was the first year any GHS football team had made it to the state championship game.

FOREST RICE

Encountering Courage

Alaska, the cold, barren wasteland, where the conditions are so harsh not many people could thrive, and only the strongest and smartest survive, such as my Uncle Shaun. So here he was, 17 years old, with only himself to rely on, being flown in on a Twin Otter, with a backpack containing a few belongings, a tent, a handgun, and some food and water. He decided to go to this specific river where he knew fishing for King Salmon was abundant. Though he could not even begin to suspect the danger fraught night he would encounter, his experience would teach him courage, perseverance, and patience, and how these characteristics would strengthen him.

My uncle set out to find the ideal place to set up camp. When he found the perfect site and had eaten a hot dinner over the fire, he decided to turn in, which probably saved his life. When he zipped the tent flap up and began to unroll his sleeping bag, he heard it, a low, rumbling huff, and then a snort. Something massive was outside the tent! My uncle listened, his heart pounding wildly in his chest. He recognized the sound; it was a Grizzly Bear. So here my uncle was, all alone in the wilderness, listening to the jaws of death, which could easily kill him.

My uncle decided he had two options, to get out of the tent and confront the bear, or stay in the tent and hope that the bear would leave. Thinking his options over many times, my uncle chose to stay in the tent and wait the Grizzly Bear out. As he cocked his gun, and held it tightly, he prepared for whatever would happen. For hours, my Uncle Shaun stayed up, fighting the fear in him, listening to see if the bear had gone. But it was still there. He could not fight sleep forever, and soon the inevitable happened, my uncle fell asleep.

In the morning, my Uncle Shaun awoke. He instantly knew a paralyzing and blinding fear. And, as much as he tried, he could not dismiss it. He concentrated on listening for the Grizzly Bear. There was no sound except the chirping of the birds and the gently swaying of the trees. But still, there was only one way to find out if the Grizzly Bear was there. He would have to unzip his tent door and peer out. My uncle hesitated, frozen with fright. With the image of losing his head, he gathered all the courage he could and unzipped the tent and looked out. The bear was gone, but his presence was still felt, for outside the tent, imprinted in the ground, were huge paw prints of a Grizzly Bear. And there they lay, as if in their own special way, they were my Uncle Shaun's badge of honor for being patient, having courage, and the perseverance to save his life in a situation where he could have surely died.

LEWIS LINK

When I was little, I went camping with a few friends of mine, Jimmy Hall, Jimmy Hodges, and Billy Hodges. On this camping trip, we take a jar of gas and a jar of water. The camping trip went fine, but when cooking on the fire, Billy was supposed to put the fire out with the jar of water. When he started to pour the water on the fire, his older brother Jimmy noticed it was the gas. There was a huge explosion that knocked everyone back.

From then on, they marked the jar of gas with a big GAS.

JAMES FINLAYSON

Perseverance
My Dad's story of perseverance starts in Mexico. He decided to go to a medical school in Mexico. All the classes were in Spanish. He had to take three months of classes in Spanish to learn the language. He went to a Mexican medical school for two years. He then went to the U.S. because he had the opportunity to start over at Emory, which was a better school. He restarted as a freshman and took all the classes over again. During school, my Dad got severe headaches and suffered dizziness. A few weeks before exams, my Dad was diagnosed with a brain tumor. His symptoms were severe headaches and dizziness. Even with his tumor, he took his exams and passed. He took the exams because it was not guaranteed that Emory University would let him start again if he missed his exams. When he went in the operation, he did not know if his tumor was cancer or not. He also did not know if he would survive or not. When he came out of the operation, he had one to two weeks of recovery before school. If this is not perseverance, I do not know what is. If you persevere, you can do anything if you keep trying.

ASHTON BLACKWOOD

When my dad was three years old, he was injured during

surgery in which they removed his tonsils. As a result he was unable to speak correctly. Some children teased and made fun of him. Other doctors gave him no hope. My grandmother didn't believe the doctors. She was convinced his speech could improve.

She helped him achieve this goal by enrolling him in speech therapy. My grandmother also called on a neighbor who worked at a radio station nearby. The neighbor acquired a tape recorder so my dad could hear himself. The sound of his voice angered him. Over the next nine years, he continued to read aloud and did many vocal exercises. By the time my dad entered the seventh grade, almost all traces of his speech problem were gone. One exercise he engaged himself in was reading a radio report or story. This helped him develop his love for news and radio today.

At the age of fourteen, my dad received his radio license. He later became a newscaster and host on public television. My dad still says today if it weren't for my grandmother's perseverance, his outlook on life would not be the same.

DANIEL FINLAYSON

Courage

This is a story of courage. It is about my grandmother and my great grandfather. It happened in the late 1930's in Canada. My grandmother Eileen and her father Lorne were out on Lake Simcoe, just north of Toronto. They were on a canoe trip when a storm struck. Even worse, Lake Simcoe is famous for its violent storms and dangerous waves. But she was not afraid because she and her father knew what to do. The way they got out is they paddled perpendicular to the waves. The people on the shore described the boat as coming up, then disappearing into the waves. While the front of the boat was up, the back was down. At that time, my grandmother lost her paddle because she hit only air when she tried to paddle. The paddle was quickly seized by her father and handed back to her. The only reason they got back to shore is they didn't panic, and they knew what to do.

ANDREE VILLACORTA

Once my dad was a boy who liked to play football. He did not do his homework. Just to play football, he had to understand that his responsibilities were to do his homework, to do his work not to play without doing homework. So finally, he understood what responsibility was. So he was now responsible for doing what he wanted to do, just doing it without saying anything, just do it, so my dad learn his lesson being responsible. Because everything has it time and place. He had learned to have patience. Now he is a great dad.

Patience was a little hard for my dad to learn, but he learned. After all he was just a boy who wanted to play and play. That was a little story about my dad.

ANGEL ARZATE

Responsibility

Mom: I learned responsibility from my dog.

Me: Doing what?

Mom: Well, I had a dog. I went to school, and I forgot that I
     had to feed him, watch him, play with him, walk him.

Me: So what happened next?

Mom: Well, I forgot to do all that for three days, and he
     didn't look so good. So I gave

him some food. He didn't want to eat or play. So I got
     worried. He looked skinny and then the next day, he was
     dead.

Me: Did you get upset?

Mom: Yes.

Me: Why? If you didn't even take care of him.

Mom: Well, that's how I learned responsibility.

MARIBEL VASQUEZ

My Dad's Short Story

        This story is about my dad's life when he was young.
When my dad was 14 years old, he began to be in gangs and use
alcohol and drugs. When my dad was 17 years old, he went to
prison and he stayed there 4 years and then came out. When he
came out, he met my mom and formed a family.

        My dad never listened. He treated us bad with no
respect, without kindness, and without responsibility. My dad left

to go places without caring if we ate, if we were good, getting good grades, and not knowing how we were doing. My dad kept going in and out of prison but still didn't listen. Then one day, my dad got tired of suffering through his bad moments and received Jesus Christ into his heart.

My dad began to have kindness, patience, responsibility, and courage to be with us now. My dad began going to church, praying, reading the Bible, and leading us to a good path so we won't do the same mistakes as he did.

MAYELA YEBRA

Responsibility

When I was a teenager, I worked at a house and made baby stuff. It is a responsibility to go to work. I just worked three months because my mom broke her wrist, and I wanted to go home and take care of her.

LAUREN STEWART

The Day of My Brother
The minister's house is where he went
A drunk driver is who they hit.
The church was too hard to go to,
The hardship and heartache is what we went through.
My brother was gone, and I can't see him again,
He was only twelve, and I was fourteen.

Perseverance is what I learned.

DARISHONE ELLISON

A couple of years back, in 1936, there was a really big tornado. I was still a little girl. Matter of fact, I had just turned 10 that summer. It was hot that summer. I really wasn't doing anything except sitting around the house and playing with my dog, Shelby. Every now and then, me and some of my friends would go to the creek to swim and play with Shelby, and something happened that I will never forget. Thursday, July 28, we were on our way to the creek and we saw a big old cloud of smoke and dust arise. Then the earth started to shake and I knew exactly what it was, a TORNADO! We all turned and started to run as fast as we could, but I almost didn't make it. I tripped over a hidden branch that was coming out of the ground. With the tornado right behind me, I just lost it and started yelling, but luckily, my best friend, Ebony, came to save me. Finally the tornado was over, but sadly, it killed everything in its path. It hit trailers, schools, houses, and fences, but, luckily, nobody was killed or injured badly. The people in the community pulled together to help fix the trailers and assist the nurses and doctors at the hospital. It was great because even though there was a tragedy, they pulled together and cooperated with each other to fix the community.

JOSE GOMEZ

Once upon a time there was a little nine year old girl named Janice. Little Janice Bowen went to buy a bag of Oreos. She quickly bought her cookies and went home. When Janice got home, she noticed that the bag was already open. Janice told her mom. Her mom told her to go back and tell the man who worked there that the bag was opened. Janice must have had a better idea because when she went in there, she quickly put the bag back and got a new one. Janice did not get caught, but that night, she felt so guilty that she told her parents what she did. They made her tell the man who worked there what she did and apologize. Janice couldn't go to her friends' house or ride her bicycle for a month, and that's how she learned to have integrity.

CARLA OLIVAS

I remember when I was in school, in maybe fourth or fifth grade, when some bullies were bothering a new girl in school. She was really scared of them. By seeing her so scared, I decided to become her friend. We became really good friends, but later she told me she had to move away. We lost track of each other, but I give thanks to life for teaching me a very important lesson: To be kind to everybody, even if you don't know them.

KIARA MAY

Lots of times, you guys in the 2000's don't really realize how good you got it. These days, you can do pretty much what you please because you have your parent's trust. I remember when I lost all of my daddy's trust. It taught me the value of loyalty.

It was 4:30 on a Wednesday, and it was time for our weekly Girl Scout meeting. Ms. Beverly told us that we were going on a camping trip. Boy were we so happy! We couldn't wait to be in the wilderness with the chaotic animals.

I crept into my daddy's room and asked my dad could I go. What did he say...no! Of course, he said no. He is so overprotective. I went to my mama, she said yes, but it is all about what my daddy says. What was I going to do? I wanted to go so badly. I would do anything.

I went to bed and got a plan, a plan that just could not fail. I would tell my daddy that I will be with my cousin all weekend. My cousin is going on the trip so we will be together. I will go on the trip and be back in time for dinner. That was my plan, and I was sticking with it.

Now is the plan going to work? I had prayed to God it would follow through. Besides, I was not really lying. We were going to be together. What I did not know was he actually called Ms. Beverly and asked her could she bring me home. Uh oh! I was busted.

So the plan did not work. My dad was so disappointed in me. I had lost my daddy's trust but most important, his loyalty. I asked him how could I get his trust back. He said it was gone.

So remember, be faithful. If your parent of a friend asks you not to do something, or tells you not to tell something, don't. loyalty is hard to find and easily lost.

BRITTANY NORMAN

This story is about my mother and her childhood. She was raised by her grandparents, and her aunts were like her sisters. She went to the county schools most of her childhood, until she started the city schools and started going to Gainesville Middle School and Gainesville High. She went to college in Savannah. That's where I was born. She had me in Savannah, then it wasn't safe there, so we moved back to Gainesville, and the rest was history.

JESUS AYALA

My grandfather told me a story of how he learned to be responsible:

When I was a little boy, I wanted a horse. Every morning I would see my dad leave to heard the cows. I would always ask if I could go, but he would say that I was still little, and I needed a horse. One day, I tried to follow him, but he caught me and sent me home. One day for my birthday, my dad came home with good news. He told me that his friend sold him a colt. He said that if I wanted the colt, I had to be responsible for feeding it, cleaning it, and providing a shelter for it. When he brought me the colt, I named her "Brisa". When I made her the stable, I made it big because she was going to grow, and I would not have to rebuild it. When she was big enough to ride, I played races with my cousin and friends. I would lose sometimes and win sometimes, but the biggest race I played was with my uncle's race horse. Luckily, I won. When my "Brisa" died, she left me another big responsibility, which grew up to be a black stallion which I named "Flush". My dad and I prepared him to be a race horse. He won many races. Until this day, he is still alive. The year that my grandson went to Mexico, he died.

KARINA ESPINOZA

Courageous Mother

She sat there watching her daughters fight for their lives. They had been born four months early. She wished she could help them, wished they didn't have to suffer. Everyday, she came to watch over them. She sat there, head in her hands, crying for them. It pained her to see them with needles all over their tiny bodies. Tubes stuck in their unmoving mouths. Each day for three of the longest months of her life, she watched them grow little by little. There were still big and little accidents, but in the end, it always got better. Sometimes they would be sent to special hospitals, but they always got through it. Today, they are healthy nine-month old babies. This is what taught my mother courage.

KIRSTON TAYLOR

Kindness

My dad was a little afraid when he first entered middle school. He thought that it would be great to show kindness to make friends on the first day. He would say, "Hello" or give someone an eraser if they needed one. Unfortunately, a student named Ray didn't like him very much. He would call him names and throw things at my dad. My dad would do anything to show Ray that being kind would make him a better person. Ray would bully my dad through high school, and dad was glad to get away from him when he graduated. Twenty years later, my uncle was getting married, and my dad discovered that my uncle's bestman was Ray, the guy who bullied him for all those years. Ray just looked at my dad, and my dad just went over to him and said, "You were just a foolish child." He gave him a hug. Showing kindness, regardless of how he treated him, would change his life forever.

MATTHEW FULLER

Horror Tornado

It was like any other day, she said, but something was tingling in her stomach. She just thought that it was a stomachache. The year was 1936, and she got up and sat up, and she was just thrilled because she could smell the sausage and eggs cooking in the kitchen.

She ate and ate her breakfast until it was time to go. Her

mom walked her to the door, and she dropped all her books. She said mom look at that. Her mom stopped and panicked. She said what do we do? The tornado is almost here.

She got all her kids and scrambled into the basement. She was in horror when the tornado came and wiped out our house with wood and brick, except the basement. She wondered did God really save us from this tornado? She thanked God so much. She and her mom and kids looked around and all the people left had their jaws to the floor. And everything was destroyed except the basement. That's all my grandmother said about the horror tornado. That is what they called it that day.

KAYLA ANDERSON

The first day of school was very scary! I was only five years old, and I was going into the first grade. As my daddy was driving me to school, I asked him, "Daddy, why do I have to go to school?" He replied, "Therese, you need to go to school to get smart."

When we arrived, I was so nervous! My palms were sweaty, my legs were like Jello, and my stomach was doing cartwheels. The first thing I saw when I stepped out of the car was the darkest forest green doors I've ever seen. The paint was chipping slightly, and as I opened the doors, I noticed the floor of the school. It was an ugly brown and the floors were so shiny and rubbery! It looked like flexible brown glass. I grabbed my daddy's hand as we began to walk. I followed at least a footstep behind him so that I couldn't be seen.

It felt like we had been walking for hours when we reached my new classroom. There was a handful of children in the room, all of which looked about my age. Then as my father began to speak my insides began to do what it felt like, twenty-four different gymnastic routines all at once. My father said, "Sister Catherine," and she came over to the door. He continued, "This is my daughter, Therese Stewart, and she will be in your class. She will not be in here today, I'm afraid, but she will be here tomorrow. I am going to take her home so that she can play."

After a couple of minutes, we left, and I got to go home and play the rest of the evening. My daddy showed kindness and love towards me. And I love my daddy greatly too.

Chris Cantrell

I help somebody I like. Helping people, I try to do what people ask me to do. Overall my definition is to be more helpful and kind. I help some with chores and parents with job. Yes some did and some didn't, but the one that did we got along well. Yes I would teach others by showing them how and helping them understand the reasoning. I learn that when you help someone by cooperating, you make good friends and can be very helpful.

LIZBETH OTERO

My Mom

Hi. My name is Velia Lazaro Otero. I was born November 11, 1964. I went to school in Mexico. I only got to the ninth grade. I could've gone to college, but I didn't because I had to help my dad with the crops. In school, I studied English and other subjects.

I got to the U.S. when I was 24 years old. I ended up in California. It was Santa Barbara, where my brother is. I met my children's daddy there. I had Lizbeth at the age of 25. I worked in a nursery of plants, and my husband worked in a restaurant and a grocery store.

After living in California for 3 years, we went to Mexico for a while. Then we went to Arkansas and lived there for a long time. It was snowing there almost every single day. I worked in a place where all I did was move boxes.

JAVON HILL

Hi. My name is Shirley. I was born Jan. 2, 1962. I grew up in G'ville, on Floyd Rd. When I was a child, where I grew up, we still had dirt roads. We had our own garden. My granddad hand raised hogs. We picked, canned, and froze most of our food from the garden. We had apple trees, pear trees, plums, peaches, and blackberries all on our property. We didn't have to go to the store for much. We had most of it at home. There were 2 houses where we lived, ours and my grandparents' house. We lived on the hill and gram and grampa, Joey, Vickie, Patricia, Bernice, and Dexter lived with gram. My mom and dad had 5 kids, me, Sam, Shell, Shryl, and Tim, and we all played together everyday. We would go to the creek to fetch water. The creek was deep in the woods. My granddad would get his gun and the dog, and we would go to the woods to fetch water from the creek. We would play in the woods, and we had lots of fun down in our little hole on Floyd Rd.

MICHAEL CHRISTIAN

Well, when I was younger, my brother and I were poor. We barely had anything to eat, and we didn't really have anything to wear. We took turns wearing clothes of each others. We went to school at Rockwild Elementary School. We stopped going at the age of eleven because of money problems. Life was hard back in the day because there were lots and lots of struggles and hard times. One thing I learned through my younger years was respect. I learned this from my favorite R&B singer, Aretha Franklin. I learned respect also by people showing it to me, and I respected others through my younger years.

MATTHEW SHIPMAN

She went to a catholic school. It was located in Anniston, Alabama. She went there for about three years. She said her and her sister were there together. She didn't remember any of her teachers. She said they had to wear the plaid dresses, and most of the time, she wore long white socks. When they got in trouble, she said they had two choices. They could get a paddling or call their parents. She said she always called her parents, because when they got a paddling, it was with a big wooden board. I asked her about their lunch, but she said she took her lunch everyday. She said when she got into the 9th grade, she wanted to go to public school with her friends, so her parents made a choice to let her go.

SHI STUDIVANT

School was different in the 60's. The education was different. They had less people in the class. They didn't have a high education advantage like we do now. In fact, they didn't even have kindergarten. There were black and white schools until 7th grade. They had somewhat a class when they were taught to respect their elders in Sunday School. Today, we have more extra-curricular activities. Back in the 60's, they only had cheerleading, basketball, and football, etc. Today, things are more computerized. Today we need about 28 to 32 credits to graduate, when they only needed about 15. Things sure have upgraded throughout the years. That concludes my interview.

KUNAL LAHIRY

Far away in another place in time there lived a man named Hirin, a brave man who was looked up to by his fellow villagers. Hirin, who was Hindu and lived in a small Indian town, was approached by the men in his village to help rid them of a terrible tiger who had been attacking sacred livestock. He agreed to lead a group of men to track down the tiger, taking a gun for protection. One of the men brought along a sword instead, thinking that he could slay it instead of shooting it. His name was Rajesh. The other men brought along guns. They looked in the forest for the dangerous tiger very cautiously, for the tiger may jump out and attack. "Look over there!!!" A man whispered to Hirin. Out of the man's excitement, the man shot at the tiger accidentally. The tiger got fightened and ran into the rice fields, where women and children still worked, not knowing that their lives were in danger. Hirin jumped up and ran into the rice field, shouting and waving for the people to clear the area. In a rice field, the grasses are extremely tall, and Hirin couldn't see the tiger anywhere. The tiger unexpectedly jumped on top of Him. Luckily, Hirin had not forgotten his gun, for he shot the tiger in the jaw. The tiger got scared and again ran into the forest. It jumped on Rajesh and tried to bite him. Fortunately, the tiger's mouth could not open and close because of the shot jaw. The man got scratched up and frightened, but nothing severe. Rajesh always brought a gun from then on if he was to hunt down another tiger like that. The tiger later bled to death from the bullet to the jaw. This took courage from Hirin because he could not know where the tiger was because of the rice field.

SHAQUEATA WALLER

Hi! My name is Shaqueata Waller. I am going to tell you a story about when my mom was my age, and she learned about different responsibilities. She was responsible for many chores after school. She was responsible for doing the laundry.

She usually had two or three loads a day. Then she had to clean the house. Once the house was clean, she had to start dinner. She had to do all of this, while making sure her little brother and sister stayed out of trouble. She also learned cooperation. She had to cooperate with her older sister in order for all the chores they were responsible for to be finished by the time their parents came home. She usually cooperated easily and got everything done before her mom and dad got home. She was also done and got paid about $5.

JOSUE FLORES

I have learned a story of courage for my grandma. Long ago, me and your dad went camping out in the woods near the river. Then a bear came out of the trees for a sip of water. You dad was scared of bears because one day at school, he saw a movie of a bear eating meat. The bear left because it was full of water. We went climbing a mountain, and it got so dark you couldn't even see your hand. The lamp turned on by itself, and we made a camp to sleep. The next day, we went on the trail. Your father was so tired by one o'clock because we woke up at five PM, so we had to rest a long time. The trail started to become steep. We took out our hooks and started climbing. At night, we went camping at the campsite, and then all of a sudden, a dog came out of nowhere and took our meat. I went out to look for the dog. Your father noticed that I was missing. He was really scared. He started crying. A while later, he forgot everything and went to look for me, and he found me.

ANGIE HIGHSMITH

Integrity
Back when I was almost four,
My mom took me to the Dime Store.

Everything was fine and dandy.
Then I spied the rack of candy.

As mom took out her billfold,
I hid in my pocket a Tootsie Roll.

When my mom saw me chewing it,
She instantly threw a great big fit.

I went inside and did what was right,
I tried not to cry with all my might.

I still remember it, you see,
The day I learned of integrity.

LUIS VIERA

My mom says that she found her courage when we were
born because she didn't want to show fear in front of her kids. So
she started to get braver and braver. That's why I admire my
mom because she has a lot of courage inside of her. I am so proud
that she's my mom. But someday, I will repay her for all she did

for me. So that's how my mom got her courage and I hope we never see my mom feeling down or really sick because I know she's pushy but she still my mom. That's what they do, so I still love my mom and my dad too because he takes care of everybody.

ANDREA ALLEN

My mother is a very courageous woman. She went to Mexico several years ago with a medical team to operate on children with birth defects. My mom's team traveled for hours into the mountains of Mexico. Families would walk for days for a chance that their child could be helped. The medical team had to decide which children could be helped.

These children had birth defects of their faces. This type of birth defect is called cleft lip or cleft palate. Mom said they worked from early in the morning until late at night, usually 12-14 hours a day, trying to help as many kids as she could. Mom said it was very hard work, but that everyone wanted to stay longer because they didn't want to turn anyone away.

My mom said she learned a lot on that trip. She learned how good it feels to help other people. Her experience taught me a lot, too.

LAURA CARMON

My mom was taught all of the character words in many different ways! Her mom and other family members taught her in different ways. Her mom taught her the words cooperation, kindness, respect, responsibility. Her mom was a great impact on her life. She was always there for her and her brother and sister.

My mom went through high school and had many friends and was a cheerleader and had good grades. She graduated and went on to KNAPP. That taught her responsibility, diversity, perseverance, and patience. My mom then went on to get married and have a baby (my older sister). My father then went into the service, and they got an apartment.

My mom then went on to do great and wonderful things and had my brother and I. Now my mom is so wonderful to me and so many other people.

ANNA KATHERINE FISK

Sitting down, he began to remove his shoes. The long day of labor had filled him with weariness. The ashes from the fireplace hit my eyes as the fire grew with intense heat. Mamma came in the room from the kitchen, "The roof has caught on fire and I got to take the shingles off," Pa calmly declared. "I reckon sparks from the chimney landed on the roof and started the fire. I got to get those shingles off to keep it from spreading so fast." We all pondered on what had just occurred. It had come as a shock to me, being only seven; I had never experienced such an incident. Mamma told us to hurry outside while daddy got on the roof to pry off our wooden shingles. I took my brother's and little sister's hands, and we ran through our tall-grassed back yard. By the time we reached the neighbor's house, I could see the fire spreading. I took off, running back to the house. Mamma and my brother asked the neighbors to come help. I noticed the flames were singeing daddy's shirt. I don't even think he noticed it because he was so focused on saving our house.

Neighbors ran inside and out trying to save the last bit of furniture we had. By now, the whole house was in flames. I stood there watching everything that we owned, our reports and memories, burn. I collapsed, overwhelmed with grief; I felt sorry for my family and for myself. We walked down the old dirt road to my grandmother's house and spent the night. I couldn't sleep. Her squeaky house smelt of aged cinnamon. It wasn't the same as home. Feeling abandonment, I went to my brother's room. We cried all night.

At daybreak, I got out of bed and went to the kitchen. I looked in the old wooden pantries for something to eat. After fixing breakfast, I decided to take a walk and ended up going home. Daddy had gone earlier that morning to feed the animals and check on the barn and farmland. On my arrival, I discovered strangers working on our house. I tried to help, but my daddy sent me back home. All that day I thought about how caring it was for people we barely knew to partake in such an act of kindness. In less than two weeks, our house was finished. It was beautiful. Everything was different, but it still felt like home.

RAYANNA JONES

My mom moved in with her grandma when she was five, after her mom died. They had to share rooms because her grandma lived in a one-room apartment. When my mom was seventeen, she had my brother. Her grandma always nagged and fussed at my mom about everything.

"You are not holding him right. That's not the way you suppose to feed him. You need to cover that baby up," she would always say.

One morning, my mom got out of bed, and the baby woke up and started crying. Her grandma woke up from the baby's loud wailing. My mom tried to hurry up and rock the baby to sleep, but her grandma was already awake.

"What are you doing to that baby now?" she said. "Stop bothering him. Rock him back to sleep!" My mother grew impatient with her fussing.

"Stop trying to tell me what to do with my baby! I can handle him on my own. We don't need your help!" Then, she took the baby and went in the kitchen. Later on, my mom felt bad about yelling at her grandma. She wanted to tell her but didn't know how.

The next day, while my grandma was asleep, my mom went to buy her a card. The card was to tell how important she was to her. So that afternoon, my mom was waking her up to give her the card, but she wouldn't wake up. So my mom called the ambulance, but they told her it was too late. She was dead.

That day, my mom said that she learned a very important lesson. That is to show kindness and respect to others, while you still have the chance.

CLAUDIA GONZALEZ

I am Maribel Reyes. At the age of 13, I worked in my house kitchen. I made food for my 5 brothers and 4 sisters. I didn't get paid making food for my brothers and sisters. I didn't go to school either, because I was poor, and we didn't have money to pay for my schoolbooks. So, during my childhood and teenage years, I never went to school. You could go ahead and say I never went to school. At the age of 19 is when I had my first child, which I named Jose Calderon. I worked in a store putting things in order and at the cash register. The thing in my life I will never forget is when I lived in San Antonio, CA. There was a grand party and that day by surprise an orchestra showed up. That is a day I will never forget. Two of the jobs I worked were housekeeping and dry cleaning. I am from El Salvador. I migrated to the United States, and I went back to El Salvador in the year 1999. While I was in El Salvador in 1999, my 2 children sent me money. I sold food and handmade tortillas. Life over there in El Salvador is hard. I had to get up every morning around 3:00 AM. I think the word that relates to my story is kindness because throughout my whole life, I have learned to always be kind to others.

KAREN MEDINA

When my dad was young, he learned how to be responsible because he and my grandfather used to do the work around our house in Mexico. There is this job that my dad had to do with my grandfather. My dad was about 14 or 15 when he did this job. He and my grandfather used to build brick houses. That was his responsibility. Every time that my dad forgot or did not bring the right tools, my grandfather would get mad, but over the years, my dad learned a lot of things, and that is why he knows everything. Now he is showing my brother what he learned. My brother is very happy to learn the responsibilities that my dad learned. But my dad is not the kind that screams and shouts. Well, that is how my dad learned responsibility.

DANG PHAM

My mom was patient when she was about to have a little baby brother. She was excited about him.

How my mom learned patience was because she waited for a long time before she could ask for a toy. She wanted an Easy Bake Oven but could not afford one because of the baby.

My mom also learned responsibility. She had to change the baby's diapers. And when her mom and dad went to work, she had to take good care of him.

Today that baby is all grown up. He also has a baby of his own, and now he has to take care of him.

KENDRICK HARRIS

Sharon was in school one day and didn't do her work. Her mother was contacted by one teacher. Sharon never knew about it. While walking home with her little brother, Kareem, they laughed and joke. She thought nothing would go wrong today. Kareem, going and putting down his books and going to play football, left Sharon in the house to do her work. Her mother came into the room and asked her what happened at school. Sharon, never looking up from her book said, "Nothing special." Her mother told her the teacher called and for her to explain why she didn't have her work. Instead of doing what she was asked, she started back-talking. Her mother let her slide for the first couple of minutes. Then she walked into another room while Sharon was still talking. She came back with a belt and punished her. She learned it was her responsibility to do her work and to respect her elders.

TOMELIA BARNES

My mom hared with me several incidents about how she learned good characteristics. My mother is the oldest of five girls. She had to take care of her younger sisters while her mother (my granny) went to work and Technical School. My mother was ten years of age, and she had leaned to be focused on what she was doing and not on other things. She cooked for my aunts and took care of them when they were sick. Now my aunts come over to my house just to taste my mother's delicious cooking. They also respect her a great deal. Responsibility is one of her good character traits.

My mother had a job as a cashier, and people would leave several items. People sometimes would leave keys, money, give too much money, or leave their change. So my mother would always return their money and the other belongings they would leave. That taught my mother to be loyal.

My mother was taught through her job about diversity. People would just throw the money at her and look at her in hateful ways. One day, she decided to tell the people who did those things that they should treat people how they wanted to be treated. From that day on, she never had to be treated like that again. Now she has friends of different cultures and hangs out with different races.

My mother's mom (my granny) made all of her kids say yes ma'am and no ma'am. So when all of my granny's kids (including my mother) grew up, they continued to use their manners. My mother or my aunties have never used profanity in front of my granny still today. They give her a lot of respect.

A fire occurred in my mother's childhood community. My mother's community had to work together and gather food and clothes for the people that stayed in the apartment that burned down. So she had to give away some of her clothes, even though she didn't want to. She had to cooperate, and that is what she did.

JASMINE MAYS

This is a story about integrity. It was a hot summer day. My mama ran a small food vending business, and she needed some sodas, so she went to the store. Se was on her way to work and didn't have much time.

When she went into the store, she got ice, sodas, and a few other items. The cashier made a mistake on the amount of sodas she had bought, and given the time, Mama never noticed that she didn't charge her enough.

When mom got to work, she discovered the mistake and knew that she had to go back to the store to make things right because of her belief in being honest as she was taught from a child by her parents.

After work, she went back to the store. She told the manger what had happened. He was surprised at her honesty and he didn't know what to say. So he thanked her and told her most people wouldn't have been that honest. She told him that God would get her if she didn't do what she knew was right.

My mama's honesty showed a lot of integrity. She could have let the store lose money and make a profit on the cashier's mistake, but she didn't. It makes you think would you have given the money back or did otherwise? This is a good story about integrity.

GLADIS BONILLA

Mi nombre es Yanira Bonilla. Y mi hermana me quieso entre-vistar ami

Esto es un a historia

Que paso en el ano 2001 en El Salvador.

Hubieron unos temblares mui fuertes que se derumbaron muchas casa y calles ce rrajaron y tamibien hubieron muchos deruumbes.

Y yo estaba en San Salvador con mi hermana

En un al bergue para ninos

Como nunca abiamos centido un temblor tan fuerte y mirabamos como se meniabatodo. I uncuch: Ilo me callo en los pieses illo pense que el findel mundo sevenia en ese momento y cuando de jode temblar pensamos en nuestra familia per que nos- abiamos como estaban

Pero gracias a Dios que todos estabamos bien

Es ta es toda mi istoria es muicorta

Respeto

You pienso que el respeto es que situquieres ser respetado tienes que respetar a los demas.

El respeto el algo que tu tienes quebalorar porque es al gomuibaliaso

Abeses mosotros no tenemos respetos

Con los demas iel respteto esque

Tenemos que respetar a las personas mayors o acual quier persona Mayor O menor

DEMESHA STRINGER

Kindness!!!

Kindness is something that you do when you're at the table, home, school. Anywhere, you should be kind. One day when I was walking down the street, I saw my friend, and she said hi. I said hi back to her. I had a big bag of snacks, and she asked if she could have one. I said yes you can have a whole pack. She said you sure are being kind. I said I know.

We were still walking and Tomelia and I saw Mary, and Mary said hey girls. We said hi. So Mary, Tomelia, and I were walking, and Mary said can I have one. I said sure. Tomelia said can I have another one. I said get one, and she got one and started walking. We walked so much that we had to sit down and eat the snacks and kept walking and then we finally came back home. When we got there, it was time to eat. They spent the night with me and had a good time.

ROSAURA RODRIGUEZ

My mother taught me to be strong and to have courage. My aunt's house was about two blocks away, and I had to take something to her. I was afraid to be brave, and it took a lot of courage. I finally walked to her house. I learned to take chances and go beyond my own yard.

Thank you to the following students and teachers who helped type the manuscript for this book:

Libby Bicknell
Manuel Burciaga
Andy Edmondson
Janeth Escalera
Tiffany Esco
Hurst Heinen
Tawanna Jackson
Mariela Jaimes
Cristi Lopez
Davis Partrick
Linet Ramos
Maria Rivas
Gaby Ruiz
Elaine Sanders
Carina Solorio
Dick Stafford
Timothy Tolbert
Stephanie Waldrip
Linda Whitley
Courtney Williams

GMS

www.ingramcontent.com/pod-product-compliance
Lightning Source LLC
Chambersburg PA
CBHW032117040426

42449CB00005B/177